TELL EVERYONE

SIM NIGER STORIES (1924-2024)

Edited by
John R. DeValve

TELL EVERYONE:
SIM NIGER STORIES (1924-2024)

Edited by John R. DeValve

Cover and Book Design by Amy G. Moore
Original photo on front cover by Joni Byker

© 2024

Publisher: SIM USA
simusa.org

ISBN: 9798336487541

CONTENTS

Introduction v
Foreword ix
Reflections on the Work of SIM in Niger xv
The 1920s 1
The 1930s 12
The 1940s 26
The 1950s 40
The 1960s 54
The 1970s 68
The 1980s 82
The 1990s 96
The 2000s 109
The 2010s 120
The 2020s 134
SIM Niger Area Director Messages 137
Timeline 150
Acknowledgements 157
Bibliography 160

Niger

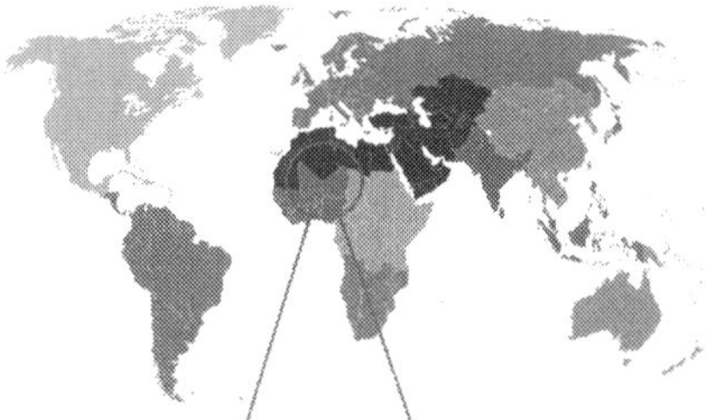

Give thanks to God for 100 years of SIM ministries in Niger!

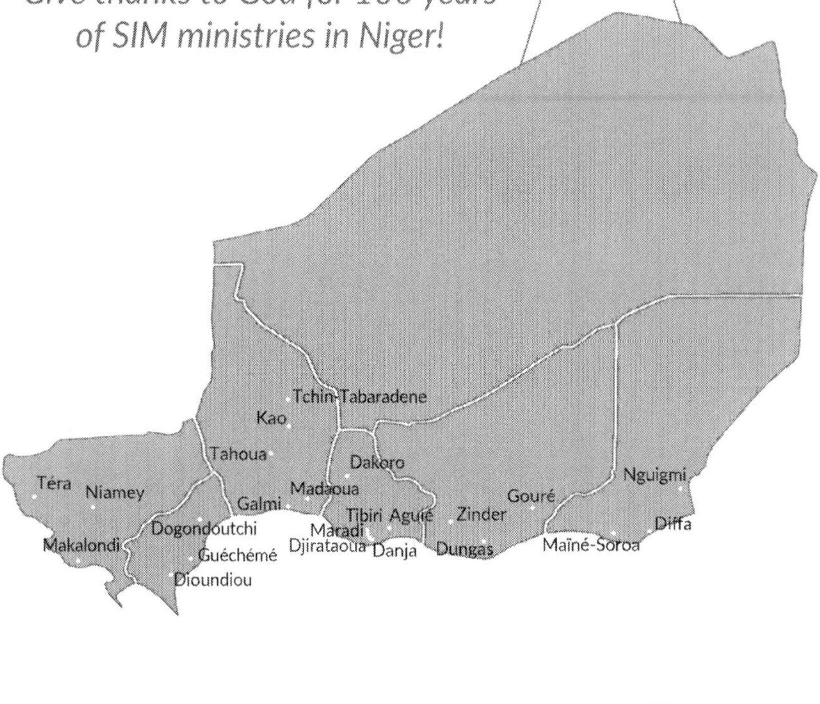

INTRODUCTION
By the Editor

SIM is an international, interdenominational, and multi-ethnic faith mission founded in 1893. Its 4000+ workers serve in 70+ countries, often not their passport country. We believe that no one should live and die without having a chance to hear the good news of Jesus Christ. Convinced of this, we are called to places where he is least known to make disciples of Jesus Christ and work with local churches to fulfill God's mission across cultures.

This book is a celebration of SIM's one hundred years of ministry in Niger from the arrival of the first missionary in 1923 until 2024. When the committee planning the centennial celebrations delegated to me the job of putting together a commemorative publication, I knew there was not enough time to write a proper history of the mission's work in Niger. Thus, I suggested that we collect stories from SIM Niger's workers and partners and group them by decade as representative samples of God's amazing work in Niger. This would involve less research and writing/editing, and the idea was born to use story to tell the history of SIM Niger. To this task I bent my mind and my fingers in February 2022.

One important consideration, of course, was that this book needed to be in two languages—French and English—because of the various audiences of the book, the multi-lingual character of the mission, and the work being done in Niger, whose official language is French. The target audience is missionaries, Christians in Niger, those who know and support SIM, and those who want to read about God's work in Niger. We want to bring glory to God by sharing what God has done through SIM and in the lives of SIM missionaries and God's people in Niger.

In an effort to keep the book from becoming too long, the stories are brief, often 500 words or less. Not every story, missionary, or ministry could be included. I have tried to include main ministries and people, but I regret that I had to exclude so many worthy stories and missionary ministries. Those who are interested may consult the bibliography, the SIM Archives, missionaries still living, or the editor for more details or depth.

One important decision that I had to make was how to spell geographical places and ethnolinguistic group names. There is considerable variation in the sources, both in missionary records and local ones, in the spelling of many geographical locations, partly because of different spelling conventions in English and French. This is particularly true for smaller towns and lesser-known places like Tibiri/Tsibiri, Guéchémé/Guéschémé, and Dandja/Danja. In most cases, I have chosen the official government spellings found on maps even if that may not reflect the actual pronunciation of the word in local languages. Thus, I have chosen Tibiri over Tsibiri and Guéchémé over Gueschémé. I have opted to keep Dogondoutchi as one word rather than write it as two because that is the way it is written on maps and signs. It is really two words, and means 'tall rock' in Hausa, reflecting the cliffs and hills in the area. Djirataoua/Jirataoua was another hard choice. I opted for the former spelling rather than the latter because, again, that is the spelling on maps. The same goes for

Tchin-Tabaraden. I also opted for the spelling Dioundiou even though the name of that town has several different spellings on signs and maps. As for Dandja/Danja, I could not find the name of the town on any map, even on the internet. I opted for Danja because most missionary sources used that spelling.

When it comes to ethnolinguistic groups, there is a great difference between English and French spellings of the names. It was difficult to choose between the two spellings since this is an English book and the French spellings are less commonly used in print for some groups. For the Fulani, the French spelling—Peul—is a completely different word. For the English version, I have opted for the English spellings for Hausa, Songhaï, and Fulani and the French spellings for Gourmantché, Kanouri, Djerma, and Touareg.

The foreword of the book is written by Dr. Joshua Bogunjoko, the director of SIM International from 2013 to 2024 and previously a doctor with his wife Joanna at Galmi Hospital at the turn of the twenty-first century. The first chapter of the book is a reflection on SIM and its work in Niger by Tounkara Maiyaldou, the current director of ESPriT, the École Supérieure Privée de Théologie (Theological College) in Niamey.

The remaining chapters follow a chronological format with stories from each decade of SIM's work in Niger. Each chapter begins with some historical information about the world, Africa, Niger, and SIM during those ten years. Following that are stories which pertain to SIM Niger's work in that decade. Some stories, of course, span more than one decade, or at least the results of the story cover more than one decade. Where they do, I have made note of that in the text. Most of the words of the stories come from the participants themselves. I have lightly edited the stories and tried to get those still living to check for errors or misstatements. Direct quotes have been set apart with indented margins, but even where there are not direct quotes, most of the words in the book are not my own. At the end of the book is a chapter of reflections from former directors followed by a timeline of key events. The timeline was mostly prepared by Beka Rideout. I have not included the entire timeline she developed. Readers who are interested can get a copy of this timeline by contacting the editor. The timeline includes events in SIM Niger on the left and corresponding world and local events on the right to give a sense of context. At the end of the book is an extensive bibliography which will be useful for those interested in further reading or research.

FOREWORD

"Tell Everyone!" These simple words from a dying man who followed the teachings of Islam all his life, then met the Savior of the world in his last months on earth, is an apt title for this book. *Tell Everyone* chronicles the incredible stories of missionaries and locals, of mission leaders and government administrators, of chaos in the world and losses in field. *Tell Everyone* is also a story that deeply resonates with my own roots.

SIM pioneers of three young men left North America in late 1893 and headed to the then called Soudan, the grassland stretching from central West Africa to East Africa. Burdened to reach this region where no one was telling anyone the good news of Jesus, the pioneers took it upon themselves to change this situation for about sixty million people. From the founding of SIM and confirmed in the many stories in *Tell Everyone* is the reality that it has always been a dangerous venture to go where no one else wants to go and to share the good news of Jesus in both physically hostile and biologically and environmentally unforgiving places in the world.

Locals have always been central to the advancement of mission work. The pioneers, assisted by a West African from Liberia named Tom Coffee, set out to reach the heart of the spiritual darkness in the Soudan—central and northern Nigeria—with a vision to see the goodness of Jesus proclaimed and lived out in Islamic Nigeria and beyond. Two of the young men died within a year, the oldest only 26 years old. Though their mission was cut short, their vision was not. The remaining young man, Rowland Bingham, returned to North America and continued to carry the flag of raising and sending workers to tell everyone.

The same commitment to tell everyone led a champion athlete from Canada, Guy Playfair, to join the mission in 1911. Playfair made his way to the small, remote village of Oro Ago in southwestern Nigeria, where he continued the tradition of telling everyone. Two years later, he made his way even further to Owa Ori Oke to preach the good news to my village and my family. The fire that was kindled in hearts starting in 1913 has not stopped burning from then until now.

In the late 1920s, pioneer Rowland Bingham traveled with two companions from Nigeria through Niger and all the way to Ouagadougou in today's Burkina Faso. Their quest? To expand the vision of telling everyone the good news while assessing needs across the region. It is quite instructive that both Rowland Bingham and Guy Playfair played a role in the unfolding story of SIM in Niger during their leadership years, and that God would, decades later, give the privilege to Joanna and I, a long-term fruit of their labor, to join the workforce in Niger to continue to tell everyone.

I have had the privilege of knowing some of the heroes in *Tell Everyone* and hearing of the incredible price paid by these and many others who came before me. Salvation is free, but the gospel goes forth at a price. *Tell Everyone* is a story of both the gift of freedom in Christ made possible through salvation, and of the extraordinary price exerted upon those who obediently carry that good news across geographic, political, economic, and cultural boundaries.

You will read of pioneering starts and even failures, yet always an enduring commitment to continue because it is the Lord who commanded us to go.

As it is today, so has it been throughout the history of SIM in Niger: the gospel crosses barriers. It has endured, survived, and even flourished despite persecution; it has stood in the face of opposition; it has weathered global recessions; it has survived a radically changing world. The gospel has endured human errors and church divisions. It has prospered through medical work and education. It has been good news of abundant farm yields and reforestation. It has lifted the stigma of leprosy and fistula. The gospel has been the source of hope for outcasts in Niger and the only source of peace for the nomads. It has torn down territorial, ethnic, and communal differences, and has brought youth together out of divided denominations.

In human terms, the stories in *Tell Everyone* should not be possible, considering the challenges of entry into Niger from an English-speaking colony to a territory controlled by suspicious French administrators. From years of application for land and for opportunity to participate in providing much-needed medical care, to the restrictions and even confinement of dwelling under an opposing government during a World War, from the high cost of lives lost—men, women, and children—to border closures that separated students from their parents in different countries and made it impossible to return home from one country to another. *Tell Everyone* is a story of the remarkable work in Niger through 100 years of God's faithfulness and the faithfulness of His people. How improbable are these stories except that we know that the One who made the promise to be with us to the ends of the earth is faithful. He is the same yesterday, today and forever.

Today, invisible lines controlled by terrorists and the threat of terrorism divide Niger. Missionaries face limitations in where they can go and what they can do. The government is fighting catastrophic environmental challenges and resulting food crisis on one hand, and terrorists who want to kill and destroy on the other. Such realities of life, if dwelt upon, would make anyone want to crawl into their beds and not go anywhere. However, the unfolding story in Niger is not one of defeat or discouragement, but of a tenacious commitment to tell everyone. It is the story of a growing work force, buttressed by new sources of mission workers from around Africa itself. Workers are now coming from regions where the pioneer missionaries moved north to start the work in Niger, workers who are as committed to telling everyone as the men and women who went before them. It is an unfolding story of leaders who, despite the increasing load of navigating new complexities, continue to urge the mission and church to tell everyone. It is an unfolding story of a missionary work force that continues to labor under the burden of uncertainty on many fronts. It is an unfolding story of churches growing in unity and participating in what God is doing and continues to do in Niger.

Tell Everyone is a two-way signpost pointing us to the past with its victories, redemption stories, pains, suffering, losses and struggles, but also pointing us to the future, urging us to learn from what God has done in the past in order that we may push forward telling everyone. We are called to continue the journey, and as you read the many stories of grace, gratitude and grinding tenacity, join SIM Niger and its workers in praise to God for what He has done and in prayer for what He will yet do. For we are convinced that no one should live and die without hearing God's good news; therefore, we believe that He has called us to make disciples of Jesus Christ in communities where He is least known. In many communities across Niger, Christ is still not known; let us re-commit ourselves to telling everyone.

Joshua Bogunjoko
SIM International Director, 2013-2024

REFLECTIONS ON THE WORK OF SIM IN NIGER

An Observation

The current sociological context in Niger is contributing to the uncertainty linked to an Islamic radicalism which has been in the Sahel region since the fall of Colonel M. Kadhafi. Movements and groups wanting to return to the practice of authentic Islam don't encourage religious freedom, or foreign missionaries, or mission work in general. When one adds to this the diminishing cooperation with western countries, one senses a rejection of the gospel, of the church, of western missionaries and of mission activity.

In light of the above, many questions come to mind regarding the future of mission in the Sahel, and in Niger in particular. A sort of general psychosis has developed among the non-Nigeriens involved in mission. Kidnappings in the region, many of those kidnapped being westerners, have pushed governments to restrict movements of westerners within the region. As a result, SIM mission activities have been drastically impacted. However, it is worth asking if the new circumstances are really the reason for a noticeable slowing of the growth of the church today.

In reading J. DeValve's writings, we learn of the history of an intense mission activity characterized by mission trips, visits to regions hitherto deemed inaccessible (for example towards Iferouâne), missionaries staying for periods in outlying villages, and efforts to produce and train new converts in collaboration with local Christians. Even if the context was different from that of today, it still presented as many difficulties as are faced today and these difficulties could have justified putting an end to that type of evangelism. What was the main factor behind the success of SIM as a mission in Niger? A look into the past will perhaps help today's church to face the challenges relating to its evangelistic mission.

Those SIM pioneer missionaries were probably less prepared than our contemporaries in their knowledge of the context into which they were heading, in their anthropological knowledge and even in the forms of communication. However, they knew how to work and produce fruit that we can still see today. We would do well to ask questions of them—through their stories—about what made their success possible. In what ways can the efforts of those first SIM missionaries help us in the pursuit of the expansion of God's Kingdom in Niger? This is a question for all who are concerned with mission in Niger, that is, the Body of Christ, and it is what J. DeValve invites us to discover in his work.

"The one who controls the past controls the future," said the British philosopher Aldous Huxley in speaking of the potential importance of history on current events. SIM's story deserves to be told. *Tell Everyone* is an exciting and edifying look back at the footsteps of the Christian mission pioneer men and women in Niger who worked under the banner of SIM. It is an honour and pleasure for me to have been invited to give my point of view on the work of SIM in Niger, as an observer. It is not my intention to add to the historical data, nor to provide a theological analysis of J. DeValve's work. First and foremost, I would like to identify all that can be useful to maximise missionary endeavours in Niger. My heart's desire is to again see the Nigerien church united as it was at first, made up of both Nigeriens and foreigners, with a view to the edification of the saints and the expansion of the Gospel.

It seems to me that missionary activity is currently wavering. By this I mean that the expansion of God's Kingdom through new converts in our churches is very much reduced compared to the times of the first missionaries. The efforts of those pioneers—of which we are the fruit—are the subject of our gratitude. There are several Christian missions in Niger, but, in my experience, none has reaped a comparable harvest to that of SIM in the great Islamic field of Niger. I welcome SIM continuing its work of producing new converts. This is a call to a new stage of mission work in Niger, using the various elements that have historically resulted in its success.

Challenges to Evangelism

As I am aware of the blockage that has affected missionary activity in Niger for some years now, it seems clear to me that mission in Niger needs to go under the microscope with the aim of adapting to the new realities and getting out to find the lost sheep. Our local churches allude to this blockage by saying "numerical growth of the church in Niger is biological," meaning that the new converts in our congregations are not coming from the non-Christian community. Evangelism from days gone by in Niger seems to be either unproductive or non-existent nowadays. In using the term unproductive, I'm implying that this evangelism does exist, but the anticipated fruit is just not there. So why this blockage? Are we doing all that we should be doing? These are legitimate questions.

As for the other suggestion that evangelism no longer occurs, this doesn't seem to be correct as we know of examples where it does exist. But is it the consuming priority for those involved? For the pioneers, "to evangelise" was a question of life or death; nothing seemed more important to them than evangelism and building up of the saints. In this context, it is appropriate to ask another question: Does the church planted by SIM, and does SIM itself, see evangelism as their highest priority today? The pioneers' perseverance is a living museum for anyone who wants to explore evangelism in Niger.

Gratitude for SIM's Sacrifice

I would like to highlight the amazing perseverance of the "Apostles of Niger" in the socio-political context in which they found themselves immersed. I want to challenge my contemporaries on the fact that the difficulties faced on the mission field were not reason enough to limit the momentum of that pioneer missionary work. In scanning what is written about the first four decades of mission in Niger, from 1923 with the visit of Edward Rice and J. Cotton to the creation of a farm school at Maza Tsaye in 1958, you see intense missionary endeavour despite the obstacles that resembled those faced by the first Christian missionaries in the Mediterranean basin. The pioneers of this work in Niger are our "Paul, Timothy and others."

Having come from other countries, they were not familiar with the local geography and had little knowledge of local linguistics, anthropology or even culture, which would have impacted on the culture shock faced by them. They jumped feet first into the Islamic jungle of Niger, with the single desire to win souls for Christ and to serve our

Lord, thousands of kilometres from their homeland. Leaving behind the comfort of technical and scientific progress, they went into regions where life resembled that of ancient times. They were exposed to sicknesses including malaria, typhoid, pneumonia, and deadly infections from any wounds suffered. Their travels were closely watched by colonial governments, they were suspected of spying for other countries, they were rejected by local enemies of the Gospel. Their zeal remained despite all of these challenges, and they stayed in Niger to complete their mission. They were ready to pay whatever the cost and made enormous sacrifices that have inspired our sympathy and respect. The greatest sacrifice that a human being can offer is the life of a loved one, or even his or her own life. Some of these "Nigerien apostles" buried their wives, lost their children on the mission field, and wives saw their husbands die of various sicknesses. Drusille Osborne, Marguerite Morrow, Evelyn Ockers, Ralph Kenneth Ganoe (aged just 30), to cite just four, lost their lives in bringing Nigeriens into the body of Christ through the mission endeavours of SIM.

Follow in the Footsteps of the "Nigerien Apostles"

What is the future of evangelism in Niger? Anyone concerned with the growth of the church amongst peoples and in regions where the Gospel hasn't been proclaimed face this imposing question: "What shall we do?" From the beginning, the field never seemed very easy, but against all expectations, souls were won for Christ through the work of SIM. At present, the mission field in Niger is still difficult and the Islamic context seems an insurmountable obstacle, to the point where some people question if evangelism is still possible.

In looking objectively at the situation, it is hard to imagine the possibility of evangelism not occurring in a social context where less than 1% confess Christ. One thing is certain, over recent decades, conversions are rarer and few new churches are being established. Since the 1990's, new churches are planted to allow existing Christians to be able to attend a church in their town or in their local suburb, or as a result of an exodus of members from SIM-related churches to join other new evangelical missions. In reality, such growth still stems from the work of SIM.

It is difficult to accept that numerical growth in our congregations through our biological families is the only way to grow the kingdom of God in Niger. The growth of the church in Niger is a great challenge to us. We are all God's missionaries in Niger, just as at the start of the mission in this country. The mission is made up of several parts, the first of which is unity, spoken of in the 17th chapter of John's gospel. The first thing to do is to live out this unity. Then come the building up of the saints and training of disciples. These are elements that can be carried out under the banner of various ministries. But the aim is singular and clear: to bear fruit. And if the harvest is small, there is a need to examine our practices to find out what is hindering the bearing of good fruit, despite our best efforts. The historical facts and the current results of the mission in Niger allow us to say very bluntly that we are the best placed of the missions to see growth in the kingdom of God in this country. It is not a matter of simply examining different mission strategies that are being used, which undoubtedly have their place. All the ministries, the training institutions, Bible schools, the health infrastructure, contribute directly or indirectly to a certain extent to the growth of the church and the building up of the saints and also enhance the unity of the body of Christ. Despite this, the key issue of evangelism, the thirst for and seeking out of new converts, needs to be examined.

This question merits consideration in order to find flexible ways and means that will lead to the continuation of the mission in Niger. It is founded on the importance of working together, as a faith community, as it was in the book of Acts and in the first decades of the mission in Niger. The collaboration between foreign missionaries and local Nigeriens was in the first instance a determinative factor in the spreading of the gospel in Niger. This wasn't just administrative in nature, but was practical, spiritual, and honest, free from any prejudice that was likely to hinder the progress of the gospel. It was founded above all on the tacit acknowledgement of the complementary nature of the various players as members of one body. In reading the contributions of Inusa Samuila, of Abba Moussa, of Dankaduli, of Dan Nana and others, one can't help but note the existence of a close collaboration. George Learned is one of those who were part of the first team that would work at a later date in the first EERN office in August 1960. This was the result of a genuine collaboration in the field, in both administrative and practical areas.

We long for a renewal in collaboration that would eliminate any prejudice, thus growing trust between SIM and the SIM-related churches. It is important to acknowledge, and to encourage, efforts to bring together the SIM-related churches and to bring SIM closer to those churches. But the current context in Niger also needs a new form of collaboration: a collaboration characterized by a spirit of fraternity, of respect and of mutual consideration. This collaboration doesn't deny our basic differences but acknowledges that those differences are less important than Christian unity. Such collaboration is able to overcome conflict and to highlight that which unites us, namely Christ. In fact, it isn't right to hurt young or new missionaries by throwing stones of rejection at them because of a hurt inflicted years ago by a missionary on a Nigerien brother. In the same way, it isn't right for expats to use stereotypical judgements to evaluate their host nation. These stigmas do not help in serving Christ. We need a collaboration that acknowledges our equality as Christians before God. This type of collaboration is attractive because it allows missionaries to stay in Niger, knowing that there are indeed missionaries ready to give their lives to save souls in Niger. Also, given that evangelism is not forbidden in the country, it allows workers in remote villages to travel anywhere for the sake of the gospel. However, local Nigeriens say they are limited by a lack of resources, not having enough to devote themselves totally to mission work. On the other hand, the expats speak of linguistic, sociological, and especially politico-religious barriers, that hinder their ability to travel freely and to settle in places that are far from the major cities. In sharing the same goals, the solution is collaboration between the two. This will be accomplished through goodwill on both sides, to allow for an evangelism where the Nigerien missionary will have the daily task of spreading the gospel, with a support that allows him to live appropriately and not as a beggar. In 2024, Niger should still be considered as a country where Christ is least known and where there is still a great need for missionaries.

Therefore, I take the liberty of repeating my heart cry, grieving the lack of new churches being planted in Niger.

I hope that this cry will be a challenge to SIM and to SIM-related churches.

>Tounkara Maiyaldou
>Director of ESPriT (School of Theology)
>Niamey, NIGER

THE 1920s

As the world recovered from World War I and the great flu pandemic of 1918-1920, there was great optimism and a sense that things would get better. New technologies like automobiles, telephones, and the cinema began to proliferate. The economy seemed to improve in some countries but struggled in others like Germany and Italy. In the US, the decade was called the roaring twenties. In October 1929, however, a great stock market crash signaled the end of boom times and the beginning of a worldwide depression that only ended with World War II.

During this decade, France, the United Kingdom, and Portugal controlled vast parts of Africa and Asia and used their position to dominate and manipulate world affairs. Meanwhile, the US slipped back into semi-isolation and xenophobia. In West Africa, there was relief as good rains returned to the subcontinent after years of drought between 1910 and 1917.

France had gained control of parts of Niger Territory in 1900. The capital of this territory was Zinder from 1911 to 1926. In 1922, the territory became the Colony of Niger, and the capital of the colony was moved from Zinder to Niamey in 1926. Niamey was then a small fishing village. Since the Niger River formed the western boundary of Niger at that time, anything in what is today's Haro Banda (including the Centre Biblique and the Riverside Sahel Academy campus) would have been in Upper Volta (today's Burkina Faso).

The first story about SIM in Niger occurred well before the 1920s but is significant because it shows the influence SIM missionaries had on Nigeriens even before they entered Niger.

The First Nigerien Believer

Probably the first Nigerien to become a follower of Jesus through the influence of SIM missionaries was Inusa Samuila. He was a Zarma from the Dosso region. Born around 1889, he made a trip to Nigeria at the age of 20 and encountered SIM missionaries in Patigi, the first SIM base in Nigeria. There he heard the good news for the first time. In 1910, he came under the influence of Dr. Andrew Stirrett, the first medical missionary with SIM. Dr. Stirrett taught him to read, and as he read the Word of God, he began to understand the truth explained in it and became a believer. In 1912 he was baptized, and in 1914 he became an evangelist, trekking over a wide area of northwest Nigeria and even southern Niger announcing the good news. He was based in Wushishi/Minna, where SIM had a large station and Hausa language school for many years. (Editor's note: Many early SIM Niger missionaries learned Hausa in Minna.) In his early years, he worked with Edward Rice, who would later become the first SIM missionary to Niger. He was still serving the Lord even in old age in the late 1950s.[1]

The First SIM Missionaries in Niger

It was during this decade that SIM missionaries made their first entry into French-held territory from Nigeria. Zinder, the capital and largest city in the colony, was a log-

---

[1] Eugenie St Germaine, "Inusa—Man of God," *Sudan Witness*, 1955, 1, 5.

ical choice to set up a first base. The work in Niger, Upper Volta (now Burkina Faso), and Dahomey (today's Benin) was under the administration of the SIM West Africa office based in Jos, Nigeria from its inception until 1972.

The first SIM missionaries to enter Niger were Ed F Rice and J Cotton. Ed Rice first arrived in Nigeria in 1904 and proved to be gifted in languages. He was extremely proficient in Hausa, the language of northern Nigeria, and his accent was so perfect, local people said that if they did not see his face, they thought he was a Hausa man. Since the British colonial authorities limited the work of SIM missionaries in northern Nigeria in the 1920s,[2] it seemed a good thing to visit Niger territory to the north, where Hausa was also the main language. So, in 1923, when J Cotton decided to visit Zinder in his Ford motor car, he invited Ed to come along. At the end of the trip, Ed felt he should stay in Zinder while J Cotton returned to Kano. Ed lived alone for several months with little money or extra clothes. A French trader welcomed him and lent him money to pay for his food and expenses. Ed was a true explorer and found it difficult to settle down in one place. He was constantly 'trekking', to use the vernacular word of the day. Here is a brief vignette from his travels around Zinder:

> I left Zinder on my bicycle with a few things fastened both to the back and front of it. The road was fairly good but rough for a bicycle in places. There was a wind that helped me along. I stopped at a rest-house for some food after I had traveled thirty-five miles. The water there was very bad. I asked the man who brought it to bring me some good water but he said there was none better.... While I

---

[2] Barbara M. Cooper, *Evangelical Christians in the Muslim Sahel* (Bloomington, Ind: Indiana University Press, 2010), 120–21.

was eating and resting the man boiled some water for me for tea. I was talking with him and he asked me some questions which I tried to answer.... I also gave him a copy of the book "Labari Mai Kyau" (Good News). He could not read it, but I asked him to take it to someone who could read it for him.

I met a soldier and his wife going to Niami (Niamey) and I gave him one or two Arabic books. He was very thankful for these, and I passed on. The road was very bad for the next twenty-five miles, and I did not have the wind in my favour which made it worse. After going twenty-five miles I had to rest for the night. The people were kind to me but seemed to want to leave me alone. When I offered a book to the malam, he sent it back saying he could only read the Koran. I was left to myself in a bit. However, the next day the people seemed more free and open with me and when I left they invited me back again.

Next day the road was bad for about thirty miles. I could make no progress at all. I passed Daura about eleven o'clock and turned into a Filani (Fulani) village. Here I rested and had a talk with some men.... These people were very anxious for me to stay with them, but I felt I must get on....

I went on and night was coming on with no house in sight. Finally, I did see some and went over but found them all occupied. However, they suggested that I go to the chief. I did and got full of burrs on the way. The chief was away and did not return till eight, so I was left under a tree outside. There were some men with me under the tree and so I talked to them, and it is surprising how they will open up as you talk to them of Christ.[3]

---

[3] Edward F Rice, "A Trip in the French Sudan," *Sudan Witness* IV, no. 6 (Jul-Sep) (1925): 22–23.

In 1924, during Ed's time in Zinder, SIM bought a property from the trader who had loaned him money. It was a big, two-story French-built structure near the center of town. Ed Morrow, a SIM missionary, who later served in Zinder for 15 years, said the purchase of this house was a mistake because it set the missionaries well above the people.[4] The house became the first base for SIM's work in Niger. By the time of the house's purchase, Ed Rice had been joined by Mr. and Mrs. Arthur Lee, the first of a string of SIM missionaries to live more permanently in Zinder.

During Ed's time in Zinder, he met Abba Moussa, who will figure prominently in the story of SIM work in Niger in the next chapter. He spent many hours talking to Abba, often lying on his bed. Ed was not in the best of health and had to leave on home assignment in 1925. He returned to Zinder the following year, but he was too much of a pioneer to remain there for long. In 1928 and 1929, he lived in Tibiri, the town that is the subject of our next story. Then in 1931, he made a long trip by camel from Kano with another missionary as far as Iferouâne in northern Niger. He was one of the first white men to visit this town in the desert. Returning via Agadez, he proceeded to Niamey and traveled down the Niger River in a pirogue to continue his work in Nigeria. He died in Minna, Nigeria, in October 1939.[5]

---

[4] Edward M Morrow, "Recollections of Mr. Edward Morrow, Sudan Interior Mission, Missionary to Niger 1930-1945," 1980, 1.
[5] Edward F Rice, "Zinder," *Sudan Witness* V, no. 3 (Nov-Dec) (1932): 5–6; Edward M Morrow, "Abba Musa of Zinder," *Sudan Witness* XXII, no. 4 (Oct) (1946): 20; "Obituary for Mr. E. F. Rice," *Sudan Witness* XVI, no. 1 (Jan-Feb) (1940): 18; John Ockers, "History of SIM Work in Niger—1923-2000," 2005, 7; Bruce E C Dipple, "A Missiological Evaluation of the History of the Sudan Interior Mission in French West Africa 1924-1962" (DMiss, Deerfield, IL, Trinity Evangelical Divinity School, 1994), 18.

Tibiri

In 1927, SIM missionaries started a second work in Niger at Tibiri, a town of about 3,000, located 180 miles west of Zinder and seven miles from Maradi. The town of Tibiri was the capital of the Gobir Hausa people, a subgroup of the Hausa nation. The Gobir had resisted the *jihads* of Usman dan Fodio in the early nineteenth century. The Hausa people in this area were more influenced by traditional practices than in other parts of Niger. Tibiri means island in Hausa, and at that time both Maradi and Tibiri were located in a river valley along a seasonal stream which comes up from Katsina, Nigeria and eventually empties into the Sokoto River in northern Nigeria. Tibiri itself was situated between two beds of the river so that it could be surrounded by water in a particularly wet rainy season.

An initial survey trip by the Playfairs—Gordon Playfair was then the West Africa director of SIM—and David and Drusille Osborne, who were new missionaries, occurred in February of 1927.[6] The trip took the two couples as far north as Tahoua. After that trip, a letter was sent to the governor of Niger requesting permission to set up residence in Tibiri. The letter from Gordon Playfair reads, in part, "I have the honor of requesting your kind permission for the Sudan Interior Mission to reside in the Maradi Circle, for religious purposes only."[7] Permission was granted, and David and Drusille Osborne moved to Tibiri on 25 December 1927. The chief of the Gobir warmly welcomed them, and they were given lodging in one of the chief's houses on his

---
[6] Ockers, "History of SIM Work in Niger," 12; "A Short History of Tibiri Station," 1947, SIM Int'l.
[7] Guy W Playfair, "Demande d'autorisation de résider dans le Cercle de Maradi," May 18, 1927, SIM Int'l.

compound near the center of town. During the next few months, they constructed a house in which to live and then left on furlough in August of 1928, leaving the work in the hands of Ed Rice and a new missionary, Hugh Rough.[8] During the 1920s and 1930s, Zinder and Tibiri remained the only places where SIM had any work in Niger.

Rowland Bingham's Trip across Niger to Ouagadougou

An exciting adventure that occurred at the end of the decade was an exploratory trip in Francophone Africa made by Rowland Bingham, one of the founders of SIM, two SIM Niger missionaries, and a Canadian businessman. While Bingham was never able to remain in Africa for any length of time after two earlier failed attempts, he was able to make several trips to Africa during his lifetime. He came back in 1929 to address the missionaries at their annual conference and then to travel across French-speaking country to determine some of its needs and assess where to place missionaries in a line from Maradi to Ougadougou. David Osborne, who had just returned from his home assignment, accompanied him on the trip, driving a new Ford touring car. Ed Morrow, who had just arrived in Africa after six months of French study in France, served as interpreter for the group.

They set out from Tibiri in late December 1929 and traveled about 200 miles a day over bumpy roads. David Osborne described a subsequent trip over the same ground in 1932. He said that once the bustle of preparation was

---

[8] Drusille Osborne, "Letter from Drusille Osborne to Mr. and Mrs. Trout," February 11, 1929, SIM Int'l; "A Short History of Tibiri Station," 1947; Ockers, "History of SIM Work in Niger," 12; Immie Larson, "A Discussion of Church Growth Among the Hausa People of Niger," December 31, 1995, 3.

David Osborne (on the right) preaching to villagers on his epic trip from Tibiri to Ougadougou in 1929-1930. Henry Stock, a Canadian businessman, is on the left. Photo captured by Rowland Bingham.

over and the travelers were in the car, there was a sense of relief and relaxation for everyone—except the driver. According to Osborne,

> He must keep on the watch continually. Wherever there are [people] in Africa, there are goats, and wherever the goats are along the roadside, whether they are peacefully lying down or grazing, they suddenly decide, when the car reaches within a few yards of them, that they must at all costs cross the road, and a mighty dash is made by fathers, mothers, and kids. One appreciates the dexterity with which the feat is performed, but frequently the wily goat is too slow and the brakes must be applied with all speed and strength to avoid collision. In some places cattle are plentiful and these

lazy, long-horned creatures will calmly stand in the middle of the road and gaze with innocent curiosity at the coming motor. Honking the horn seems to have the effect of petrifying or mesmerizing the solid bovine which usually obliges speed-loving man to slacken up to a walking pace or stop altogether, and then [they] saunter off as if the whole incident were a huge joke....

We drive up a fertile valley frequently passing by villages and hamlets. Then comes a stretch of more barren and unproductive country. Perhaps there are hundreds of square miles with no human inhabitants. Here wildlife abounds. As we speed along, we come upon a small group of graceful, dainty gazelle who gaze intently for a few moments with their large, black, lustrous eyes, and then with a toss of the head they bound off to shelter....

In the first four hundred miles of our trip there are several points where the road takes a sudden dip, and we pass through what is obviously an old water course possibly fifty feet deep and a quarter of a mile wide. Doubtless centuries ago these were mighty tributaries of the lordly Niger. Today [locals] dig in these old channels wells that are upwards of two hundred feet deep, to secure water for their flocks and herds. At another point we pass a number of strange looking hills of curious formation. The first thought is that they are extinct volcanoes, but close observation indicates the awesome fact that we are in the bed of what was once a huge lake, and these hills are nothing but islands of hard rocky soil that were not worn down by the process of erosion.[9]

---

[9] David M Osborne, "Travelling in French Sudan," *Sudan Witness* V, no. 1 (Jul–Aug) (1932): 8–11.

There were no Christians or missionaries along their route until Niamey, where the African Christian Mission —later the Evangelical Baptist Mission—had recently been established. Once in Niamey, they had to go through customs and cross the Niger River. At that time there was no bridge across the river, and once on the other side, one passed into Upper Volta as the border was the Niger River. Here is how Osborne described the passage:

> The end of the second day finds us at Niamey, the seat of government of the Niger Colony. Here we have to go through the formalities of inspection of passports, etc for we are soon to enter the Haute Volta Colony. At the one and only "canteen" (general store) we replenish our supply of gasoline and drive down to the river's edge and await the ferry— a small pontoon with outboard motor attached. Careful driving is required to bring the car up and on to the ferry. All secured, we are piloted across the Niger, which at this point is about five hundred yards wide, but very uninteresting as it slowly rolls along between the brown banks.[10]

The party traveled on to Fada N'Gourma and ended up in Ouagadougou. The journey was significant for several reasons. First, it was one of the first trips by SIM missionaries across what was then little-known territory. Second, it marked the beginning of SIM work among the Gourmantché people. Third, upon reaching Ouagadougou, Rowland Bingham made an agreement with the Assemblies of God (AoG) mission that SIM would work among the Gourmantché while the AoG would confine their work to the Mossi. Fourth, the SIM work among

---

[10] Ibid., 10.

the Gourmantché was soon to become part of the work in Niger when eastern Upper Volta was absorbed by Niger in 1932. The Gourmantché work was administered by a superintendent in Maradi until 1972. Finally, it showed some possible locations for future SIM work in Niger as well as revealing limitations that might accompany the work.[11]

---

[11] Larson, "A Discussion of Church Growth," 3; Rowland V Bingham, *Seven Sevens of Years and a Jubilee: The Story of the Sudan Interior Mission* (New York: Evangelical Publishers, 1943), 91–92; Edward Morrow, "Beginnings of SIM Work at Zinder, Niger," January 31, 1987, 1; Dipple, "A Missiological Evaluation," 26–28.

THE 1930s

The decade of the 1930s was a time of a worldwide economic crisis and depression. SIM workers often found it hard to raise the support necessary to do their work, and they often had to spend more time in the home countries raising that support, but the work continued. By the end of the decade, World War II had started in both Asia and Europe. Of course, the war left a significant mark on the world but helped to bring an end to the world economic crisis.

During the decade, the town of Niamey, founded in 1902, began its growth as the capital of Niger Colony. As the administrative center of France's work in Niger, the town was divided into two sections, one an administrative, French sector, the other, an African, residential sector. The dividing line was the Gountou Yéni, the stream that bisects the city and runs beside the finance building and between the museum and the Noom Hotel, emptying into the Niger River behind the Palais des Congrès. There was no bridge across the Niger River until the Kennedy Bridge was built in 1970. To cross the river, one took a ferry. The old ferry slip is on the Corniche Yantala below the National Hospital.

The colony of Upper Volta, founded in 1919, was dissolved on 05 September 1932 as a cost-cutting measure by the French colonial authorities. The eastern part of Upper Volta, including the towns of Fada N'Gourma and Dori, became part of the colony of Niger. This meant that

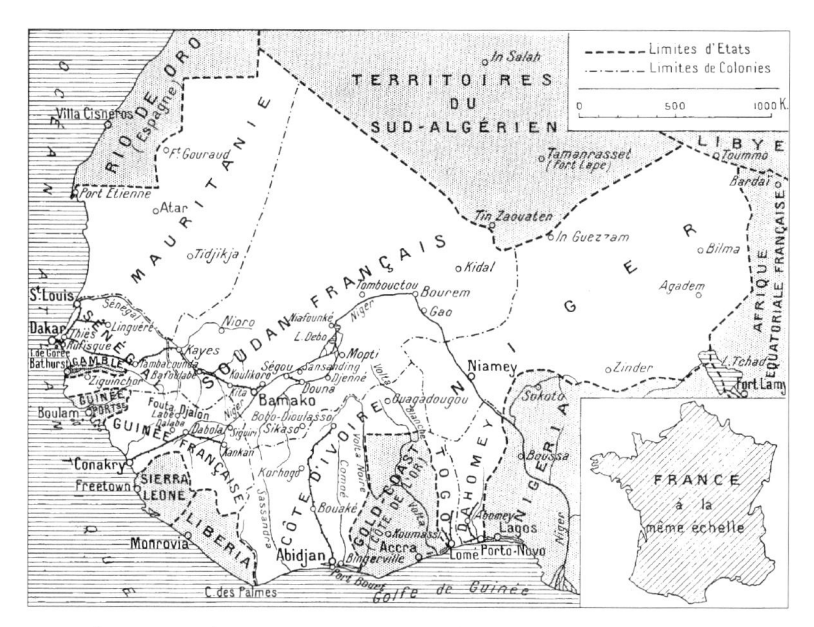

French West Africa c. 1936. Note the western border of Niger extends to Togo and Côte d'Ivoire. (Map in the Public Domain)

most of the Gourmantché region was under colonial administration of Niger until 04 September 1947, when the colony of Upper Volta (today's Burkina Faso) was revived with its current borders.

SIM Niger in the 1930s

During the 1930s, SIM Niger was not able to expand beyond the three centers of Zinder, Tibiri, and Fada N'Gourma. The mission applied to the colonial government to enter Tahoua, Galmi, Dogondoutchi, and Diapaga, but permission was not granted. The government also refused permission to start leprosy work.[12] Not until 1940 did SIM

---

[12] Guy W Playfair, "Retrospect and Prospect," *Sudan Witness*, 1936, 1, SIM Int'l; Newton Kapp, "Survey in French West Africa," *Sudan Witness* XXIX, no. 1 (Jan) (1953): 19; Addo Mahamane, "Chapter 8: History and Challenges

work expand to two other locations in French-speaking West Africa near Tibiri: Maradi and Djirataoua. During the decade, the band of missionaries never numbered more than 20—often less than that—but before the end of the decade, work was well established among the Hausa, the Touareg, the Gourmantché, and the Fulani.

Feet of Clay

The early Niger missionaries were imperfect human beings and made many mistakes. While we may look up to them for their vision and example and laud them for their strength and courage, they had feet of clay. Ed Morrow was one of these early missionaries. He arrived in Africa in mid-1929, and the West Africa field council assigned him to Tibiri to work with a single missionary, Hugh Rough. Ed was extremely happy with this assignment and expected to have a successful ministry amongst the Hausa in Niger. Reality hit hard very quickly, however. In his later years, Ed Morrow admitted that he and his fellow missionaries made numerous mistakes and failures in their work. The first failure he mentions occurred during the exploratory trip Rowland Bingham made across French Africa (see the previous chapter). Here is Ed's description of his role in that trip as a new missionary:

> I was asked to go along on that trip as interpreter for Dr. Bingham.... There were four of us who set out in Mr. Osbourne's [sic] car. We stopped at every government station where I had to interpret

---

of the Evangelical Church in Niger, 1923–2013: The Case of the Evangelical Church of the Republic of Niger (EERN)," in *Transforming Africa's Religious Landscapes: The Sudan Interior Mission (SIM), Past and Present* (Trenton, NJ: Africa World Press, 2018), 227–28.

(I did the best I could).... I must confess from the very beginning I trembled in my shoes because my French wasn't very much after only six months in France.[13]

One question that could be asked was why the traveling group did not include Drusille Osborne, David Osborne's wife. She was French Canadian and the best French speaker amongst the Niger missionaries. Why risk earning a reputation as poor French speakers with the authorities, a reputation later imparted to these 'Anglophone' missionaries which may have started with this trip?

After his return from the epic journey, Ed Morrow was assigned to work in Zinder with Hugh Rough. Hugh did not stick it out there, but after marrying Marguerite Ross in August 1930, Ed and his wife served in Zinder until 1945. Ed relates what happened to them during their first term:

> We were not prepared intellectually, spiritually, and physically for this work.... We did not know anything about Islam.... Children were forbidden to come on the compound.... I was ignored.... All we could do was simply to go out amongst the people visiting.... Marguerite lost weight. She had been ill.... We went home early [in 1932 in the midst of the Great Depression] because all of this was hard on Marguerite.... We left with a broken heart because we did not know if our work had any worth in Zinder. Why were we suffering so much?... At first, we told our Mission superior that when we return back to Africa that we didn't want to go back to Zinder. But God had His will for us in Zinder. [He] led us to read Samuel Zwemer's and Lillias Trotter's books [Zwemer and Trotter

---

[13] Interview with Ed Morrow, July 1985, 1, SIM Int'l.

worked among Arabs in the late nineteenth and early twentieth centuries]. Their books were helpful, and we felt that we had a burden for Muslims. We wrote letters to our supervisors that we now understood we should indeed return to Zinder.[14]

It seems that there was insufficient preparation or training for early missionaries other than Bible and language training. While there can be too many conditions imposed on new missionaries, training in cross-cultural communication, understanding Islam, how to face hardship, and anthropological principles could have been helpful for people like the Morrows. Today, we are more aware of this need, but we need to continue to be learners and prepare for the work to which God has called us.

Abba Moussa

One of the remarkable stories of God's grace in the lives of Nigeriens occurred during the 1920s and 1930s and continued in succeeding decades. When Ed Rice went to Zinder in the 1920s, he encountered a man named Abba Moussa. The last chapter referred to their relationship and how they debated in Rice's room during his brief time in Zinder.

Abba Moussa, born at the beginning of the twentieth century, was a keen, intelligent boy whose father was an 'al haji' (someone who performs the pilgrimage to Mecca). He was put in Qur'anic school to become a malam (Qur'anic teacher), but he rebelled against his parents and ran away from the school multiple times. His father chained his leg

---

[14] Morrow, "Beginnings of SIM Work at Zinder, Niger," January 31, 1987, 3; Interview with Ed Morrow, 2; Morrow, "Recollections of Mr. Edward Morrow, Sudan Interior Mission, Missionary to Niger 1930-1945," 1980, 2.

to a stake in the school yard, and Abba remained a virtual prisoner at the school for two years. Later, he studied at an Islamic university in Bornu (northern Nigeria).

Abba Moussa never became a malam but instead went to work for the French authorities in Zinder. Learning of his intelligence, they shipped him off to Niamey to a government school. Over the next two years, he gained a good working knowledge of French and studied other subjects. He also learned to drink alcohol and became a habitual drunkard.

On his return to Zinder in late 1924, he learned of the stir caused by the arrival of two Christian missionaries. They were Ed Rice and Arthur Lee, mentioned in the last chapter. Abba went to meet them. He became a language helper to Arthur and later to Ed Morrow. Arthur gave him a Bible in French, and Ed Morrow gave him a Bible in Arabic and a Hausa New Testament. Abba began to read and study the Scriptures methodically and debate with the missionaries about religion, religious practice, and faith.

When Ed and Marguerite Morrow arrived in Zinder in 1930, they had frequent contact with Abba Moussa. Ed, who was about the same age as Abba, counted him as a close friend. For nine years, Abba searched the Scriptures, studying and comparing them with other things he had read and studied. One night he dreamt that he was in a large, dark room, so dark that he was afraid. He saw someone approaching him dressed in black. He awakened in fear. Then he fell asleep and had another dream. This time he was in a room with a beautiful light. He felt peace. He saw someone approaching dressed in white, shining clothes. The person seemed to be the source of the light. He knew it was Jesus.

By the end of the decade, Abba Moussa had confessed faith in Jesus Christ. He stated that it was not the preaching of the missionaries that brought him to the light, but the Word of God speaking to his heart. He gradually stopped drinking, and he decided to plant his crops in the shape of a cross. Two big events on his farm happened in the 1930s. One rainy season, as he looked outside, he saw locusts filling the skies. He cried out to the Lord to save his crops, and when he went to his fields the next day, they had been preserved even though all around was eaten. In another rainy season, lack of rain was threatening to kill his crops. He fell down on his knees, and while he was praying, he heard the sound of rain coming. Looking out of the house, he saw a dark cloud over his fields. Rain fell on his crops, saving them from the drought.

Abba Moussa suffered opposition, particularly when he tried to preach in the open air over a microphone. At one point his house burned down, and he lost all his precious books, but he remained firm in faith. In later years, he had disagreements with the Zinder church, and his life was not always exemplary, but before Ed and Marguerite Morrow left to start a work in Dahomey in 1946, he prayed in their hearing, 'God, if you see me going back to darkness, kill me. It is better that I die than to go back into darkness.' All of his children followed him in his faith, and many of them served the Lord in various capacities in the church and civil service of Niger.[15] One of his sons-in-law was Harouna Labo, later president of the Evangelical Church of the Republic of Niger (EERN).[16]

---

[15] Morrow, "Beginnings of SIM Work at Zinder, Niger," 1, 3; Morrow, "Recollections of Mr. Edward Morrow," 1980; Morrow, "Abba Musa of Zinder"; David M Osborne, "Outline of Mission Work in Niger Colony," *Sudan Witness* XXII, no. 4 (Oct) (1946): 8; Ockers, "History of SIM Work in Niger," 8.
[16] Mahamane, "Chapter 8: History and Challenges of the Evangelical

Dan Kundule

Another story from Zinder concerns Mamane Dan Kundule. Hired as a laborer for the remodeling of the house in Zinder, he later became a houseworker for the missionaries. After learning to read and write, he started reading the Bible. One day, he stated that he wanted to follow Jesus. After the Morrows left Zinder, they sent him to Kano Bible School. When he returned to Zinder, he was a pastor and became the first licensed minister in Niger on 06 June 1959.[17]

A Trip Up the Niger River

None of today's missionaries have traveled in a pirogue (canoe) on the Niger River as their primary means of transport. This story comes to us from John F Hall, who traveled up the river in 1932 from Jebba, Nigeria as part of his journey to Fada N'Gourma to work among the Gourmantché. He writes that he traveled with a companion, a Mr. Stanley, from Jebba to Gaya, Niger. Since there were no outboard motors at the time, they had to laboriously paddle and pole over the rapids in the Niger River in the area where today's Kainji Lake exists. The Kainji Dam, completed in 1968, dammed up a large section of the Niger River, creating a massive lake covering the rapids that had existed there. It was there in 1806 that the Scottish explorer Mungo Park met his demise when he jumped into

---

Church in Niger, 1923–2013: The Case of the Evangelical Church of the Republic of Niger (EERN)," 250, 255.

[17] Morrow, "Recollections of Mr. Edward Morrow, Sudan Interior Mission, Missionary to Niger 1930-1945," 1980, 3; Mahamane, "Chapter 8: History and Challenges of the Evangelical Church in Niger, 1923–2013: The Case of the Evangelical Church of the Republic of Niger (EERN)," 234.

the rapids to flee pursuing locals who were trying to kill him. In any case, the dam provides electricity to many communities in West Africa. Here is John's account of the remainder of the journey on the Niger:

> To me fell the job of getting another canoe at Gaya. In answer to prayer, we had already [met] men two days below Gaya who wanted the job. After a long palaver in Hausa, I succeeded in bringing down the price from one thousand francs to three hundred and fifty. The three men who poled were of the Dandawa (Dendi) Tribe and spoke Hausa well. They became very interested in the Gospel and made opportunities for me to preach in towns on the river. It was pleasant to travel with them, for they knew every nook and cranny of the river from Gaya to Say.… It took ten days to Say, so that altogether I was thirty-three days on the Niger! At Say, two of the boatmen came to me quietly and said they believed in Christ and wanted to follow Him. One added, 'But what shall we do? There is no one in our tribe to teach us.' … I still find Hausa useful and have had the privilege several times of preaching the Good News to those who understand. I am not yet proficient at [Gourmantchéma].[18]

Tibiri in the 1930s

The work of SIM in Niger continued in Tibiri for the entire decade. Many missionaries lived there, the response was greater than in Zinder, and the activity of the mission was concentrated there. The French colonial authorities were suspicious of SIM's work, however, for two reasons:

---

[18] John F Hall, "Farthest West," *Sudan Witness* V, no. 3 (Nov-Dec) (1932): 11-12.

the missionaries weren't Catholic, and they were mostly anglophones. Anyone who knows the rivalry between France and the UK over the centuries will understand the doubts the colonial authorities had as to the real intentions of the missionaries. At best, they were treated with mild respect. At worst, they were suspected of being spies for the British. During the decade, the authorities forbade SIM missionaries from conducting medical work without trained medical staff, and they put a stop to a school because it wasn't in French and had no teachers trained to French standards[19]. Another obstacle to mission work in Niger was the large deposit required by the authorities for the repatriation of a body in case of death.[20]

Still, the work did go on. People began to respond to the message the missionaries presented. The first baptisms were held in Tibiri in 1930 with four people baptized. A Sunday School was started for teaching children. Local believers were trained in presenting the gospel and sent out to preach. Most of the first believers were from the noble class. They were often immature in the faith and were easily influenced by the chief and the traditional leading families. One early convert from the chiefly clan, Janjuna, was enticed to revert to traditional ways and renounce his faith to receive the chieftainship of a newly created locality.[21] It was not until after World War II that commoners began to turn to Christ in large numbers.

One story of people's response came from a boy in the Sunday School. One night he was so ill that he could not

---

[19] Cooper, *Evangelical Christians in the Muslim Sahel*, 162–63, 166–67; Drusille Osborne, "The Growth of the Sunday School at Tibiri," *Sudan Witness* VI, no. 5 (Mar-Apr) (1934): 13.
[20] Dipple, "A Missiological Evaluation," 22, 144.
[21] Ibrahim Nomaou and John R DeValve, Tsibiri dans les annees 1930-1970, Face-to-face, February 3, 2024.

sleep. Refusing to let his mother sacrifice the usual black goat for his recovery, he asked his younger brother to pray with him. His prayer went something like this: 'O Father, you know that I have not been able to sleep all night because of pain. If you will, please give me sleep.' The two went back to bed—they slept in the same room—and the suffering one went sound asleep and slept into the afternoon with no other ill effects. He experienced the sufficiency of Christ to meet his need.[22]

Credit to Local People

It is important to give credit where credit is due. A great deal of the real work in the 1930s (and subsequently) was carried out by local believers who preached the word and testified of their faith. They were more effective than the white missionaries in gaining a hearing. This is what one might expect as their command of the language and customs of the people were far better than any outsiders. As a Zarma proverb states, 'a floating log never becomes a crocodile'. While one might have inside knowledge and look like an insider at times, it is difficult for a stranger to become an insider to another culture.

Examples of this abound. Dan Daura, an evangelist with the Church Missionary Society in northern Nigeria, held a series of meetings in Tibiri and surrounding locales in 1931 and 1933 which produced much fruit.[23] Another example was 'Dan Nana Dodo, a man who came from a commoner background but had a powerful influence on many. He was among the Nigeriens baptized in 1930 in

---

[22] Osborne, "The Growth of the Sunday School at Tibiri," 14.
[23] "History of Tibiri Station," 1933, 3, 5, SIM Int'l; Ockers, "History of SIM Work in Niger," 13; Dipple, "A Missiological Evaluation," 21.

Tibiri and traveled widely to preach.[24] Later, a local man named Garba Guidimouni was a very effective apologist for the gospel in Dungas.[25] One woman who is frequently overlooked is Tashibka. She was an early believer from the former slave class. An elderly, illiterate woman in Tibiri, she exerted a powerful influence on the nascent church through prayer, oral arts, and a letter she dictated in 1949 urging more white Christians to come to Niger as missionaries.[26] The efforts of these witnesses must not be glossed over or forgotten. The church of today rests largely on their shoulders.[27]

The Touareg People

SIM began its work in Niger among the Hausa, but it wasn't long before some missionaries saw a need to minister to the nomadic Touareg people. This group had resisted French rule until 1922, and it was only after the resistance had been put down that Niger became a separate French colony under the French West Africa administration.

The first SIM missionaries to work among the Touareg were Ken and Naomi Hodgson. They arrived in Africa in 1932 and were soon engaged in Touareg ministry. Here is a brief narrative of Ken's trip to visit some Touaregs in the Zinder area.

---

[24] "History of Tibiri Station," 3; Martha Wall, *Splinters from an African Log* (Chicago: Moody Press, 1960), 277–78; Cooper, *Evangelical Christians in the Muslim Sahel*, 170–71.
[25] Dipple, "A Missiological Evaluation," 69.
[26] Cooper, *Evangelical Christians in the Muslim Sahel*, 190–91; Ockers, "History of SIM Work in Niger," 16; Tashibka, "An African Letter," trans. Ray De la Haye, *Sudan Witness* Supplement II 3 (May) (1949): 3; Thelma Kephart, "Ray and Sophie de la Haye: 41 Faithful Years," Intercom, October 2009, 165 edition, SIM Int'l.
[27] Nigel Younge, "SIM in Niger: the origins and development of an Evangelical Protestant church in Muslim West Africa" (Chester, UK, University of Chester, 2015), 49.

We loaded our camels and set out on a route unknown to us. It was late in the season and water was often scarce and very filthy. For four days we traveled over dusty, dry plains, followed along dry river courses and passed over rugged hills, and at length we arrived ... The chief is a man of influence. Many visitors from even greater distances dropped in, and here we met past acquaintances and strangers. Many were the informal meetings and interesting discussions over the Word of God. We spent nearly three months there and when we were obliged to leave, the Touaregs turned out in force to bid us farewell and urged us to return.[28]

In an article for the British edition of the *Sudan Witness*, Ken Hodgson lists some of the unique characteristics of the Touareg ethnolinguistic group:

1) They do not build houses or sow seed.

2) They have a cross-like symbol embedded, woven, welded, burnt, or cut into most of the things they possess. Of the twenty-one crosses which symbolize the various locations and clans of the Touareg, the Agadez Cross is the most famous and serves as a symbol for Niger.

3) Unlike the Arabs, it is the men who wear veils.

4) Their writing system is unique and older than any other currently in use in the world.

5) They are camel, sheep, and goat herders, traveling from place to place in search of water and sustenance.

6) The live in the Sahara, one of the most inhospitable places on earth.

---

[28] Kenneth O Hodgson, "Visit to a Touareg Camp," *Sudan Witness* IX, no. 3 (Nov-Dec) (1935): 19.

7) They transport goods via caravan across the desert. They also used to raid caravans and tax them.

8) They are generally matrilineal, tracing their genealogy through the mother.

9) Unlike many Muslims, monogamy is the general rule for them.[29]

---

[29] Kenneth O Hodgson, "Men of the Veil," *Sudan Witness (British Edition)* VII, no. 3 (Nov-Dec) (1960): 1–2; Kerry Lovering, "Rugged Life Among the Tuareg," *Africa Now*, no. 59 (Jul-Aug) (1970): 3; Ockers, "History of SIM Work in Niger," 66; Kerry Lovering, "The Nomad Tuaregs, Islam's Lords of the Desert," *Africa Now*, 1978, SIM Int'l.

THE 1940S

By 1940, Europe and Asia were already at war, and on 22 June 1940, France fell to the invading German forces that had already overwhelmed Denmark, Norway, the Netherlands, Belgium, and Luxembourg. In the wake of the German victory, the French were permitted to set up a semi-autonomous government loyal to the Nazis at Vichy in the center of France. The Vichy regime advanced a strongly Catholic position and collaborated with the Nazis. The French colonies in Africa split over allegiances. French West Africa (Senegal, Mauritania, French Soudan, Côte d'Ivoire, Togo, Dahomey, and Niger) sided with the Vichy regime while French Equatorial Africa (Chad, CAR, Congo, and Gabon) and Cameroon sided with the Free French under Charles de Gaulle. This meant that Niger fell under the authority of Vichy France, and, by extension, the Nazis. French West Africa remained on the side of the Germans until the Free French took over West Africa after the Allied invasion of North Africa in November 1942.[30]

SIM went through big changes during the war. The first general director, Rowland Bingham, died in 1942. There was an interim period where his deputy, C. Gordon Beacham, served as acting director, but in 1944, Guy William Playfair became the new general director. He was the West Africa field director from 1917 on, and he was to serve as general director until 1957. The international

---

[30] Cooper, *Evangelical Christians in the Muslim Sahel*, 244; Dipple, "A Missiological Evaluation," 33.

office of SIM was then moved to Jos, Nigeria, and 'home' offices were established in North America.

Because most of the 15 SIM missionaries in Niger at the beginning of the war were anglophones and Protestants, they were viewed with utmost suspicion by the French authorities and treated like enemy spies. Their movements were restricted, and the border with Nigeria was closed, cutting them off from information and medical help as well as the possibility of rest and relaxation.[31] The district superintendent, David Osborne, was even arrested and taken to Niamey where he was detained for several weeks in late 1942.[32] It was not until June 1943, after the Free French assumed control of West Africa, that the missionaries were freed from restrictions and could move about freely.

Just before the start of the war, the work expanded to two locations in the Tibiri area: Maradi, at the instigation of the authorities, and Djirataoua, south of Maradi.

Unfortunately, the missionary family in Djirataoua was forced to move to Tibiri a few months later so that they could be under the surveillance of the colonial government which had just aligned with Vichy France. The first missionary house in Djirataoua is pictured on the next page.

Just after the war, in 1945, SIM was permitted to return to Djirataoua and to start work in two new locations: Diapaga, in the Gourmantché region, and Dogondoutchi, to the west of Tibiri, to work with the Maouri (or Arewa, a term that means 'north' or 'children of Ari') Hausa subgroup. Later, in 1948, SIM also began work in Madaoua.

---

[31] Cooper, Evangelical Christians in the Muslim Sahel, 230–31; "French West Africa," *Sudan Witness* XVI, no. 5 (Sep-Oct) (1940): 24; Larson, "A Discussion of Church Growth Among the Hausa People of Niger," 3; Ockers, "History of SIM Work in Niger," 16.
[32] Younge, "SIM in Niger," 42.

This humble dwelling at Jiratawa is the new home of Rev. and Mrs. de la Haye, who are in charge of this newly-established outpost in the Tsibiri area.

Source: Sudan Witness

Illness and Death

The 1940s were a time of great upheaval, tension, and sorrow. Among the most discouraging and heartbreaking events SIM missionaries faced during this difficult decade were the serious, incapacitating illnesses of SIM members and their children and the sudden death of several missionaries in the prime of life. One of the most upsetting and disheartening of these events occurred in late 1940 after France had fallen to the Nazis. By October, SIM Niger missionaries were forbidden to leave the colony and had minimal contact with the SIM field headquarters in Jos. On October 7th, Drusille Osborne became ill with double pneumonia in Tibiri. She was already suffering from an infected hand. Though attended by a French doctor from Maradi, she died four days later of blood poisoning and pneumonia. The news did not reach Nigeria until early 1941 as the telegraph lines between the countries were not working properly due to the war. The message first reached SIM headquarters through a trusted Christian courier who traveled surreptitiously across the border with a memorized message for the SIM leadership.[33]

Drusille Osborne's death was not the only tragedy of the decade. In October 1947, Maguerite Morrow, who had served faithfully with her husband Ed in Zinder for 15 years, died after a brief illness. The Morrows had just transferred to Kandi, Dahomey, to begin a work in the north of that country, but even though they were not in Niger at the time, the loss was keenly felt.[34] Then on 26 June 1948, Ralph Kenneth Ganoe died suddenly of pneumonia. He and his family had recently arrived in Africa and moved to Djirataoua, which had not had resident missionaries since before the war. He was thirty years old.[35]

In addition to these losses, there were serious illnesses recorded among the missionaries and their children. Ray de la Haye was evacuated to Nigeria with typhoid in 1947. He barely survived.[36] In 1948, Jean Osborne, twin daughter of David Osborne and his new wife Marie, suffered a wasting disease as a result of severe dysentery and was left paralyzed and helpless for the remainder of her life. Though she returned to Africa after some medical consultations in the US, she had to be constantly cared for,

---

[33] Ibid., 42; Cooper, *Evangelical Christians in the Muslim Sahel*, 234; Guy W Playfair, "Obituary for Drusille Osborne," *Sudan Witness* XVII, no. 1 (Jan) (1941): 3.

[34] H A Kirk, "Obituary for Marguerite Morrow," *Sudan Witness* XXIV, no. 1 (Jan) (1948): 12–13.

[35] Alberta Simms, "SIM Niger in the 1940s," December 4, 1992, 5, SIM Int'l; "Obituary for Ralph Kenneth Ganoe," *Sudan Witness* XXIV, no. 6 (Nov) (1948): 7–8; Wall, *Splinters from an African Log*, 244–46.

[36] Simms, "SIM Niger in the 1940s," 2–3; Wall, *Splinters from an African Log*, 225–27.

and the Osborne family had to cope with an invalid child in addition to their mission responsibilities. She died just before her ninth birthday in 1956.[37] Martha Wall, a nurse recruited to work in the dispensary in Tibiri, had to return to the US earlier than her scheduled furlough in 1950 due to exhaustion and fatigue, leaving the dispensary in the inexperienced hands of Rita Salls and Alberta Simms.[38] Later, in 1949, the de la Hayes lost one child to cancer, and a second child suffered a speech impediment when he contracted meningitis.[39]

Smuggling of Messages to Nigeria

Communications between Nigeria and Niger were limited during the war, and telegrams were often not sent or delayed. In addition, the movement of SIM Niger missionaries was restricted. Because of this, the missionaries occasionally sent clandestine messages across the border with Nigeriens who could move about freely. One was the messenger who related the news of Drusille Osborne's death, related in the last section. This messenger was none other than 'Dan Nana Dodo, one of the first believers in Tibiri, who appeared in the last chapter. 'Dan Nana was a prominent believer who preached and testified in many towns and villages in the Maradi area. Furnished with a vehicle by David Osborne during the war, he posed as a Hausa trader and crossed the border plying tradition-

---

[37] Wall, *Splinters from an African Log*, 240–41, 247; Simms, "SIM Niger in the 1940s," 5; David and Marie Osborne, "Prayer Letter," August 1949; Dipple, "A Missiological Evaluation," 72–73.
[38] Simms, "SIM Niger in the 1940s," 3; Wall, *Splinters from an African Log*, 249–51.
[39] Wall, *Splinters from an African Log*, 247–48; Ockers, "History of SIM Work in Niger," 18.

al medicines. His real purpose, however, was to transmit messages from the Niger missionaries and bring back news of the outside world to them. He had to memorize the messages, as it would have been dangerous to bear written messages with him. In this way, the missionaries were able to communicate with mission leaders in Jos and Kano.[40] 'Dan Nana went on to attend the Bible School at Tibiri and was part of the early leadership of the EERN. He composed a letter to mission supporters which appeared in the *Sudan Witness* in 1947 and reported on a trip he made to Tanout (southeast Niger) and the opportunities for gospel witness in that region. His plea at the end of the letter was for more workers.[41]

Shipwreck!

Charles (Zeb) and Irene Zabriskie started out their missionary careers with SIM in Nigeria in the 1930s. They were married in 1939 and spent their next term working in Kano Province. In 1943 they were on their way home for furlough in the middle of World War II. Their ship was part of a convoy that zig-zagged across the Atlantic to avoid being torpedoed. They were one day out of New York when about midnight they were awakened by a terrible crash and a splintering of wood. They thought they had been torpedoed, but it turned out that another ship in the convoy had hit them. They had gone through several lifeboat drills and knew what to do. Since they were sleeping with their clothes on, they grabbed overcoats

---

[40] Cooper, *Evangelical Christians in the Muslim Sahel*, 233–34; Younge, "SIM in Niger," 41–42; Playfair, "Obituary for Drusille Osborne," 3.
[41] Dan Nana, "A Letter from Dan Nana," trans. Ray De la Haye, *Sudan Witness* XXIII, no. 3 (May) (1947): 15.

and made their way to the boats. Their ship sank 12 minutes after the crash. After what seemed an eternity but was only three hours, they were picked up by a ship in the convoy. The captain of their vessel was relieved to see them as their cabin had been close to where the ship was struck. They lost all their possessions, including Zeb's translation and linguistic notes. This incident deepened their commitment to share the gospel with those who had not heard, and when they returned to Africa after the war, they helped start SIM work in Dogondoutchi, Madaoua, and Galmi. Then they served in Tahoua sharing the gospel with Touaregs from 1951 until they retired in 1976.[42]

The Maradi/Tibiri Flood

A big catastrophe that strongly affected SIM work in Niger in the 1940s was the massive flood that occurred in central Niger at the end of World War II. At that time both Maradi and Tibiri towns were located in the valley close to the Goulbin Maradi, a seasonal stream bed that rises near Katsina in Nigeria, flows north into Niger, and turns south after Tibiri, returning to Nigeria, where it joins the Sokoto River, and eventually the Niger. Normally a dry, sandy water course, it fills with water for a few months during and after the rainy season. In 1945, unusually heavy rains caused this stream to rise far beyond its banks, inundating both Maradi and Tibiri. Tibiri, which in Hausa means island, became more like the bed of a lake. Most of the mud houses in both towns collapsed, and the inhabitants fled their homes for higher ground. Roads in the area be-

---

[42] "Obituary for Charles Zabriskie," December 10, 2001; Ockers, "History of SIM Work in Niger," 61–62; Marcia Zabriskie, *A Challenge from the Sahara* (Niger, 1984), 8–9.

came impassable, and the road to Nigeria was washed out. The SIM properties in Maradi and Djirataoua were flooded, and the Tibiri dispensary, protected by sandbags, was surrounded by water. As a result of the flood, the governor ordered the construction of new towns on the hills adjacent to the stream and forced everyone to move onto the hillside. In Tibiri, the town moved up to where the SIM property was already located and eventually surrounded it. David Osborne had predicted this flood way back in the 1920s and was hailed as a prophet by the local people.[43]

Martha Wall was a SIM missionary nurse who had spent one term in Nigeria and transferred to Niger at the end of the war. During this flood, she was travelling from Nigeria to Niger on a lorry to work at the dispensary in Tibiri. Here are excerpts from her description of the journey.

> It was August when David Osborne's urgent letter warned us that the season of steady, torrential rains was imminent, and that meant that Niger's dry-season roads would become impassable. ... The road from Katsina was poor, but not dangerous. At Jibiya [Nigeria border town], however, we found a line of lorries drawn up at the side of the road.... Nobody was even considering a crossing of the deep washout that made entrance to the bridge entirely out of the question. Mr. Abed (the truck driver) and the lad he had brought with him... waded into the stream to find the shallowest route. ... I had noted that the river, though fairly swift, was not too deep, and it looked far less dangerous to me than climbing the opposite bank by lorry. I told him that I wanted to wade the river.

---

[43] Dipple, "A Missiological Evaluation," 19–20.

There were a few very tense moments in the middle of the stream when it seemed that the lorry would bog down and remain there for the duration of the wet season. ... To the accompaniment of a great deal of grunting and shouting and some genuine shoving, the lorry finally pulled through the stream and started up the steep slope of the bank. The ascent did not take nearly as long as the crossing had done, but it was far more frightening. ... At last we were on the other side.

The road in French territory was far worse than the road to Jibiya. We detoured some spots, shot through some others with the same casual daring that had marked Mr. Abed's contempt of hindrances all along the way. Sometimes we were jounced and jolted roughly, a few other times we seemed to keep our balance only because everyone held his breath. Once Mr. Abed did slow down while his Nigerian boy found the road for us, feeling for holes, where the road was covered by an expanse of water nearly a mile wide.

Every mile brought us nearer Maradi. We had only 13 more miles to go when we plowed over a slight rise on which was built a small village. Below us lay a literal lake, miles wide. ... It became clear that no one would drive a car here for many days.

She narrates how they had to return over that broken, precarious road to Jibiya where she spent four days of waiting, looking for a way around the flood. Finally giving up, the party returned to Katsina. There she received a note from SIM people in Niger that she should travel to Jibiya the following day to meet Ray de la Haye who was coming down with a horse and carriers. They would ride the fifty miles to Maradi by a winding hill route through the bush, dodging the flooded roads. Here is her description of the journey by horseback:

> Those were hard miles...fighting to get our horses down steep banks, into streams, crossing wet [millet] fields that were surely 15 feet tall. The stalks that lashed at us were usually wet with dew or a scattered shower. By the end of the first day...I was so tired that I did not wait for the [helpers] to set up my army cot. ... We had come only 15 miles.
>
> The next day we started out in a heavy drizzle. ... Our destination was Djirataoua, 20 miles [away]. ... Even the best guide can become lost. Once...we made a great loop in our trail that lengthened our trek by at least an hour. ... We reached Djirataoua fairly early in the afternoon...and it was still early enough for us to ride on to Maradi, which was only five miles from Djirataoua. ... Ray would send one of our [helpers] on to Tsibiri ... [and] Mr. Osborne would come in his car [to get us].
>
> [But] it began to rain.... Because of the quality of dry-season roads [in French Territory], it is illegal to drive...during a rain and for 12 hours afterwards.... [Ray] felt that, under the circumstances, our wisest action would be to ride on to Tsibiri, ... eight miles away!

They slogged through the night, arriving weary and sore at Tibiri after covering a two day's journey in one day.[44] The flood meant that SIM's property in Djirataoua was no longer near the new village, rendering it obsolete. Later, the Tibiri dispensary, which was in the flood plain

---

[44] Wall, *Splinters from an African Log*, 158–66; Martha Wall, "Prayer Letter," 1946; David M Osborne, "Tsibiri Flood Report," August 11, 1945; "From Tsibiri," September 1945.

of the river, was also moved up on the hill near the new town. Finally, many houses and buildings had to be rebuilt because of the rains.

Medical Work at Tibiri

Martha Wall transferred to Niger to serve as nurse in the dispensary at Tibiri. In the 1920s and 1930s, SIM Niger had wanted to do medical work to alleviate the suffering of the population and promote better health. Medical work was effective in Nigeria in sharing God's love with local people, especially at an eye hospital in Kano and leprosaria in various locations. But the French colonial government restricted medical centers in Niger that did not have trained medical staff on site. For the first twenty years of the mission's work in Niger, the government refused permission to open medical facilities.

In 1944, the French authorities relented and ceded to SIM the use of the government dispensary at Tibiri if they could staff it with trained medical personnel. At first, Marie Osborne, the second wife of David Osborne, was in charge, but by August 1945 she was on the point of giving birth to twins, and she needed help. That was what created the urgency for Martha Wall to arrive not only before the birth but also before the rains cut off the roads. The dispensary was the first official medical-based work of SIM in Niger and was a major part of SIM's work in the country until the 1960s. The dispensary was deeded to the Niger church (EERN) along with the SIM Tibiri property in 1983.[45]

---

[45] Ockers, "History of SIM Work in Niger," 15, 21; Osborne, "Outline of Mission Work in Niger Colony," 9; Cooper, *Evangelical Christians in the Muslim Sahel*, 309–18; Wall, *Splinters from an African Log*, 169–221.

Miracle Car

A fascinating story of God's kindness and providence occurred in 1946 when Newton Kapp and Ray de la Haye took a tournée (tour) around all the stations in Upper Volta, Dahomey, and Niger in Ray's old 1929 Ford Touring Car. As they were traveling between Maradi and Madaoua trailing a big cloud of dust on a road that was not much wider than a footpath, they hit an unseen object, lurched, and came to a stop. One wheel was bent out of shape. The spare was already damaged, and there they were, stuck in the heat of the day in the middle of nowhere. There were few vehicles of any kind in the country at the time, and they knew they could be there for a while. Newton looked at Ray and said, 'Well, that's that.'

After praying about their situation, they pitched a shelter, and, seeing some guinea hens off in the distance, went off to secure some dinner. As they trudged through the countryside, they came across a burned-out road building camp. There in the ashes of the camp was a blackened 1929 Ford Touring Car with intact wheels! They praised God and got out the jack from the car, unbolted one from the burned-out car, put it on Ray's car, and off they went. Had this accident occurred 300 yards in either direction, they probably would have missed seeing the road camp and the unlikely car buried in it.[46]

Bible School at Tibiri

Another initiative of SIM Niger during the 1940s was the founding of a Bible school in Tibiri. This was the only serious attempt at theological training during the first forty

---

[46] Ockers, "History of SIM Work in Niger," 19; Kerry Lovering, "Man with the Big Back Yard," *Sudan Witness* XLII, no. 3 (Jul-Sep) (1966): 2.

years of the mission's work in Niger, and it left the church critically unprepared to take the reins of leadership at independence and had a direct impact on church growth.[47] The school was plagued with problems, not the least of which was the dearth and cost of building materials after the war. After it opened in early 1947, its director and teacher, Ray de la Haye, fell seriously ill with typhoid and had to leave for several months. Instruction was in Hausa even though the colonial administration wanted French literacy with a secular curriculum. The choice of language also limited the possibilities for employment of students upon graduation. Classes were held on weekdays with ministry on weekends. The school started promisingly with nine students, but it never graduated more than thirteen. It closed in the 1950s but was revived in 1963, when it was moved to Aguié.[48]

Building the Church in Tibiri

The building of the church in Tibiri is an exciting story. Up until 1945, the believers met in a storage shed on the mission compound, but those facilities became crowded, and the local believers wanted more independence from the mission. In 1947 Moussa Marafa, a member of the chiefly clan in Tibiri, donated land for the new church, and work began making bricks and preparing materials for the construction. The chief and local people opposed the construction, however, and tried to stop it first by vandalizing building materials and second by complaining to the commandant in Maradi. The commandant, not wishing to

---

[47] Dipple, "A Missiological Evaluation," 99–100, 118–20.
[48] Ockers, "History of SIM Work in Niger," 18; Younge, "SIM in Niger," 49–50; Wall, *Splinters from an African Log*, 222–26; Dipple, "A Missiological Evaluation," 45.

antagonize the local people, initially sided with the chief and his supporters, but when the believers protested his decision, he relented and allowed the construction to proceed. The believers said that the initiative for building came from themselves, that the building was to be constructed on private land, and that they had as much right as any other citizens to have a place of worship of their own.

Work on the church began in earnest just before the rainy season of 1948. Construction was delayed so long that the building was still unfinished when it was time for the planting rains to start. The heavy rains would have destroyed the mud building without its roof, rendering all the work to that point worthless and postponing the construction until the dry season six months later. The Christians prayed. Rains fell in many of the surrounding communities, but not in Tibiri. The Christians continued to pray, and the rains held off. They held off so long that everybody in the area was getting anxious and praying for rain. Without any help from the missionaries, the Christians pursued the construction with vigor. People who had opposed the construction soon joined in so that the rains would not be delayed any longer. When the church was finally completed, the Christians held a thanksgiving service, and that night it poured. It rained so hard that one corner of the uncured roof of the church collapsed without any real harm to the rest of the building.[49]

---

[49] Ockers, "History of SIM Work in Niger," 13-14; Wall, *Splinters from an African Log*, 227-34; Cooper, *Evangelical Christians in the Muslim Sahel*, 191-96.

THE 1950s

The decade of the 1950s was a time of optimism and hope. World War II was over, and the world had recovered from the depression of the 1930s. The tension of the Cold War, however, left many people caught in the middle between the two main nuclear powers, the US and the USSR. War flared in Korea for three long years. During this decade there was also the space race, a dramatic increase in world trade, and the beginning of commercial jet travel, which started to shrink the distances between the corners of the world. Increasingly, missionaries and diplomats traveled to their posts by air rather than by sea.

For Africa, the 1950s was a time of rising aspirations as countries pushed for, and in most cases, achieved political independence from European domination. Libya, Sudan, Morocco, Tunisia, Ghana, and Guinea were the first countries to arrive at this milestone. Most of Francophone Africa joined the French community of nations in 1958, with internal self-government and the creation of national institutions like a presidency and a legislative body. This event is commemorated on 18 December every year in Niger as Republic Day. His Excellency Mr. Diori Hamani became the first president of Niger (1958-1974).

For SIM Niger, there was rapid expansion in personnel, in ministries, and in the number of places where missionaries were located. Medical ministries, in particular, opened in various places. Galmi Hospital was founded in 1950, dispensaries opened in Guéchémé (1953) and Dungas

(1955), and Danja Leprosarium admitted its first patients in 1956. SIM missionaries also started work in Soura—just a short walk from Maradi—in 1951 and in Tahoua in 1952 to work among Touareg people.[50] New ministries to boys and girls also began, with girls' schools in Maradi/Soura (1952) and Dogondoutchi (1954), and a boys' farm school in Maza Tsaye, just outside Maradi (1957). Because of the expansion of ministries, there was a need for an administrative office for the three Francophone countries separate from the administration in Jos, Nigeria. A business office was opened in Maradi early in 1951.[51] Gradually, most of the missionaries in Tibiri moved to Maradi to be near the administrative center. The believers also left the town for other places, leaving Tibiri with little gospel witness.[52]

Founding of Galmi

Arguably the ministry with the most profound effect on SIM work in Niger, both then and now, is that of Galmi Hospital. Opened in 1950 after fifteen years of negotiating with the French colonial government and researching for a good site, it was at the time one of only three hospitals in the country. Located on a dry, rocky outcropping in a tiny, isolated village, the hospital quickly gained a good reputation for compassionate, restorative care. Ruth Long relates how the French hoped the hospital would not survive in this barren landscape.[53] However, it turned out to be

---

[50] Younge, "SIM in Niger," 37, 39.
[51] Mahamane, "Chapter 8: History and Challenges of the Evangelical Church in Niger, 1923–2013: The Case of the Evangelical Church of the Republic of Niger (EERN)," 235.
[52] Nomaou and DeValve, Tsibiri dans les annees 1930-1970.
[53] Ruth Long, *A Family Living under the Sahara Sun* (Bloomington, IN: Xlibris Corp., 2011), 63; Larson, "A Discussion of Church Growth," 4; Lover-

a strategic location along the east-west highway traversing the country and was accessible to a large population. There are many stories about Galmi that would merit inclusion in this book. In this chapter a few stories from the early years and one story that spanned several decades will be related.

The first doctor at Galmi was Burt Long, who arrived with his wife Ruth and two children in July 1950. Already, construction of the hospital was in full swing. The hospital was in the shape of a 'T'. The Galmi compound included a house for the Long family and a duplex for two single nurses. There was no wall or fence, and early photos of the site look bare and sparse with few trees or plants. That year, David Osborne, the district superintendent of the mission in Niger, predicted that Galmi would one day become the garden spot of Niger. It's not exactly the garden of Eden today, but it is a pleasant oasis on the edge of the desert[54]. With no security, it was easy for anyone to enter the compound. Ruth Long describes one night in April 1951 when a thief stole coverings and slippers from under their noses while the family slept outside[55].

David Osborne met the Longs when they arrived in Galmi and helped them get settled. Before returning to Maradi, he quipped, 'Don't let anyone die! It will get you off to a bad start!' His words must have been a real motivation and incentive to get the care of patients right, but what pressure the Longs were under! This is especially true when one realizes that only those in the most desperate straits would visit the hospital.[56] Ruth relates how they finally overcame people's suspicions and misgivings:

---

ing, "Man with the Big Back Yard," 3.
[54] Long, *A Family Living under the Sahara Sun*, 562; Harold Fuller, "Hospital on the Edge of Nowhere," *Africa Now*, no. 33 (Apr-Jun) (1967): 6–7.
[55] Long, *A Family Living under the Sahara Sun*, 77.
[56] Ibid., 70.

With a limited supply of medicine and equipment, Burt began to see some patients. At first they were afraid to come to see the white doctor, but in desperation a teen age girl came with pus dripping from her head. This had been going on for months, perhaps years, and of course her hair was matted and the odor was not pleasing. Burt saw that the problem was osteomyelitis, a piece of bone had fractured and was trying to work its way out but could not. Burt shaved the area, made the cut, removed the piece of bone, put in a drain, and in a few weeks she was well. The ice was broken. Patients began to come.[57]

The Longs lived without electricity during their first years. They had two stoves: a wood stove—the only stove they had during their first term—and a kerosene stove they brought back with them after their first home assignment in 1954-1955. The following story concerns insects, not the earwigs which today plague the Galmi compound after the rainy season, but cockroaches, which are huge and ugly in Niger.

> We were always in a battle with the cockroaches and.... I did a pretty good job of keeping them down. One morning as I went to the kitchen to prepare breakfast, I noticed a cockroach running around on top of the [kerosene] oven. So I lit the burners and watched while the oven started to heat. As it got hotter and hotter, the cockroach ran faster and faster. Unfortunately for him, he couldn't escape. Gradually he slowed down and eventually stopped and fell over. I loved every minute of watching [his] demise. The kids thought I was sadistic![58]

---
[57] Ibid., 72.
[58] Ibid., 150.

One of the ongoing problems at Galmi was the struggle to obtain a good, reliable supply of water. While this issue persisted into the twenty-first century, it was particularly acute in the first decade of the hospital's existence. Initially, during the dry season, the Longs and the hospital got their water from shallow wells in the valley below the hospital. An adolescent boy would transport the water in large clay pots tied to a donkey and empty the pots into drums each day. These wells would collapse in the sandy soil when it rained, so in the rainy season, water was collected in drums as it poured off the roof or by skimming it from puddles and boiling it. Sometimes, the missionaries had to take barrels to the town water hole and fill them up with the tan-colored water. Later, the missionaries constructed more durable wells in the valley using concrete rings to line the wells and prevent their collapse. The water table was only 20 feet down, so the wells were not very deep. Still, those wells were a half mile away, and it was an arduous trek to get the water to the hospital and houses. In 1952, they tried to dig deeper wells on the compound. That didn't work, either. They had to dig down 85 ft, and all three wells had bad, bitter water. Another attempt to obtain a reliable water supply was to build cisterns around the homes and the hospital to collect rainwater, but these either collapsed or leaked after a short while, and the idea was abandoned.[59] Ruth Long describes a third attempt to store water that nearly ended in disaster:

> Another effort that didn't get off the ground was the tower that we built behind the chapel. That was the highest ground on the compound…. The idea

---

[59] Ibid., 70–71, 95–97, 158–59.

was to put a tank on top of it in which to store water. Then the water would flow down to the houses and hospital by gravity. [But] the tower cracked.... [The] mason repaired the tower and added 3 more feet to it to increase the pressure flow. It was all set to have the tank raised—the tank holds 350 gallons. One night... [there was] a terrific storm; the next morning after breakfast, there was a... thud, and in 10 seconds the tower was completely down. Nothing but rubble.... Fortunately, the tank was never raised. More fortunately, no one was near it when it came down.[60]

Eventually, the missionaries laid pipes from the wells in the valley to the houses on the compound, storing it in barrels on platforms so that they could have internal plumbing and running water.

SIMAIR Authorization

One of the encouraging developments of the decade was the authorization from the colonial headquarters in Paris to land airplanes in Francophone countries. The letter from the French authorities is dated 16 June 1951.[61] SIMAIR had been set up in Jos, Nigeria in 1946 to transport personnel more quickly and evacuate people to hospital who suffered from injury or illness. SIMAIR did not have a base in Niger until the 1970s, but it was authorized to fly to Niger, Dahomey, or Upper Volta once a month to pick people up and take them back and forth to Nigeria, sometimes with more than one plane. This authorization helped expand the work of SIM in Niger and the other two

---

[60] Ibid., 159.
[61] "Autorisation d'atterir en AOF," juin 1951, SIM Int'l.

The first SIMAIR flight from Nigeria to Niger ready for takeoff.

Francophone countries. In the early years, SIMAIR landed in Maradi, Birni N'Konni, Madaoua, and Malbaza. The landing strip in Galmi was not constructed until 1975.

Some flights were dedicated to transporting children of missionaries to Kent Academy for their schooling. On one particularly harrowing flight, a SIMAIR plane was landing in Madaoua with children returning from Kent Academy. On the way in, the plane lurched unexpectedly. When it landed, it was discovered that it was dragging a telephone wire it had snagged just before the airstrip. The plane could have somersaulted, but everyone arrived safely.[62]

Illness and Death

In the 1950s there were several deaths of missionaries' children. One story comes from the Darling family. Don and Dorothy Darling with their two girls Linda and Beth

---

[62] Long, *A Family Living under the Sahara Sun*, 169, 247.

came to Niger in 1950 to build houses and buildings for missionaries. They were in Tahoua in 1952 helping build houses for the missionaries who would be moving there. On 9 March 1952, Linda died of spinal meningitis, after being sick for about a week. She was six and was buried in Tahoua. Just a year and a half later, the Darlings lost their seven-month-old baby Philip, probably from an overdose of typhoid vaccine. He was buried in Maradi. How anyone could endure the loss of two children in less than two years is beyond comprehension, but then so many Nigeriens face the loss of multiple children that one can become numb to death and suffering. The Darlings only served four years in Niger (1950-1954). When they returned to the US for furlough, their baby daughter Carolyn needed an emergency tracheotomy that required long-term care. They were never able to return permanently to the country although Don did travel back four times for short-term building projects.[63]

That was not the end of the serious illnesses during the decade. Ben Van Lierop, stationed in Dogondoutchi with his family, developed serious headaches in 1956. He had to be transported by road first to Galmi and then to Kano for treatment. There, it was determined to send him on to London, where he was diagnosed with a brain tumor. After surgery to remove the tumor, he was able to return to Niger for a few years, but the tumor returned, and the family was forced to go to the US for medical intervention.[64] He died on 5 November 1960. His wife Gwen continued in ministry in Niger on her own until the mid-1980s.[65]

---

[63] Ibid., 91–92, 124; Ockers, "History of SIM Work in Niger," 60–61; Dipple, "A Missiological Evaluation," 48–49.
[64] Gwen Van Lierop, "Cut and Polished," *Africa Now*, December 1964.
[65] Long, *A Family Living under the Sahara Sun*, 151–54.

Another loss was the death of Earl Playfair, son of SIM General Director Guy Playfair, in 1955. He worked in Dahomey and traveled with his oldest child, Grace, to Miango so she could start school at Kent Academy. He fell ill in Jos and died of a stroke. His wife, Jean, transferred to Niger and spent many years in the east in a pioneering ministry.[66]

Evacuation in a Bathtub

As we saw in the last chapter, Martha Wall was one of the first trained nurses at the Tibiri dispensary. After a term there, she worked at Galmi and Madaoua, then back at Tibiri, waiting for the construction of buildings in Guéchémé, where she would serve as the first nurse in the new dispensary.

While Martha was waiting, she asked for permission to live in a rural village 30 miles west of Tibiri during the rainy season. In addition to sharing the gospel and discipling, she wanted to test a new system for teaching reading that she had devised. During the 1950s many locations in Niger were very remote and isolated, especially during the rainy season from June through September. Given Martha's health history and the fact that she could be cut off by the rains, the SIM director in Niger, Newton Kapp, was reluctant to let her go by herself. The area had already been evangelized by Nigerien Christians, including 'Dan Nana, and her somewhat dismissive attitude toward the risks should have been a red flag. Nevertheless, she was given permission to go.

---

[66] Kerry Lovering, ed., "People of the Wilderness," *Africa Now*, Jan-Feb (1975): 5; Charles Truxton, *The Quiet Passion Behind the Stones* (Jos, Plateau State, Nigeria: Geovany Digital Creative Prints, 2023), 82–84.

On 22 July 1952, Martha loaded eight 60-pound head-loads into the Kapp's car, and they drove to the edge of the flooded valley, where porters would have to carry the loads across the swollen, hip-deep waters. But only one man and two boys showed up to carry the loads because everyone else was in the fields. She had to reduce her loads to three packs and ride a horse through the torrent, slipping and sliding as she went. The journey of about five miles took all day. The rest of her loads arrived two days later.

Martha stayed in the village teaching and treating the illnesses of the local people, but she increasingly began to feel ill. By the end of one month, she could barely stand or focus, and it became obvious that she needed outside medical help. She had jaundice and was vomiting after every meal. But the way back to Tibiri was cut off by swift water, and six people had already died trying to cross the stream. Finally, in desperation, the villagers decided to take matters into their own hands and transport her to Maradi by a different, longer route. Martha rode horseback but had to be held up on the horse until they got to the river. There she was deposited in the home of a hospitable Nigerien, who did everything he could to feed and care for her. Meanwhile, her goods had been transported across the river, and a messenger had been sent to the mission with news of her condition. The messenger returned with a message that she should be transported to the river at once to be picked up in the mission car. Here is her description of the end of the journey:

> [My bed where I was lying] was hoisted up on the heads of four carriers who pushed through the tall grain over uneven, slippery paths. It was dusk when I was deposited in my long, galvanized tin bathtub which had been tied, on a precarious slant, to two

empty oil drums to make a fairly seaworthy raft. Eight swimmers shouted encouragement to each other as they towed me through the swift current to safety on the other side.

Martha rested in Maradi for a week before being transported to Jos, Nigeria for recuperation at Bingham Memorial Nursing Home. She had severe liver damage from hepatitis, and this seriously compromised her further work in Niger. Though she was able to go to Guéchémé after this incident, she only stayed for a year. She left Niger in 1954 when her mother fell ill. It is always difficult to balance risk and potential benefits, but this trip put many lives at risk with meager gains. In addition, Nigeriens had already been faithfully working in this village, and they had more of an impact than the foreigners.[67]

God Provides Stone

The ground around the city of Dungas is sandy and soft. There is no rock or gravel that is suitable for building. Gravel was needed to reinforce cement, but there was none to be had. The nearest stone was over fifty miles away, too far to haul in the 1950s. The construction of a dispensary and a house for the missionaries was in jeopardy. The builders prayed that God would provide a solution.

One day as the crew worked, Gordon Bishop, who was helping with the building, was walking around in the fields near the construction site. He stumbled on something that looked like a stone. Sure enough, when the con-

---

[67] Wall, *Splinters from an African Log*, 277–302; Ockers, "History of SIM Work in Niger," 18, 52–53; Martha Wall, "Help Those Women," *Sudan Witness* XXIX, no. 2 (Mar) (1953): 7–9; Cooper, *Evangelical Christians in the Muslim Sahel*, 300–303.

struction crew dug down into the sand, they found quite a lot of rock, which they were able to make into gravel. As long as they kept digging, they kept finding more stone.

The chief of the area and government officials came to ask how the missionaries had found the stone. They didn't know there was any stone in the area. The missionaries replied they did not know there was stone there, either. They just prayed, and God provided it for them. People started coming and asking if they could have the stone when the missionaries were done with it. The missionaries replied that when they were finished, people were welcome to whatever remained. After the building project was finished, they informed the chief, the government officials, and a local businessman that they could have as much stone as they could dig out. But when those people came to the site, they could not find any stone. It had all been used up in the building of the SIM mission station! No one ever found stone there before or after.[68]

Opening of Danja Leprosarium

Seeing the effectiveness of leprosy work in Nigeria, SIM made application to the French colonial government as early as 1940 to open a leprosarium in Niger. This application was tentatively approved, but the war postponed the final approval, and it wasn't until 1952 that permission was finally granted to open the new facility. After scouting around to find a good site, a suitable location was found in Danja, some 10 miles south of Maradi, and construction began in 1953. The first patients were admitted in 1956. At that time the prevalence of leprosy (Hansen's disease)

---

[68] John Kopp, Recollections of George and Mae Beacham, February 12, 1988, 11–13.

was extremely high in the area at 187.5 cases for every 10,000 people with over 300,000 total sufferers[69]! The leprosarium has contributed to reduce that prevalence to 0.1 per 10,000 people in the country of Niger, with about 304 sufferers in 2021, according to the WHO[70]. Not only that, many of the patients at Danja went on to live productive lives.

Because leprosy patients often had to spend months or years in Danja, they had prolonged exposure to Christian teaching. Many of the followers of Jesus in Niger today trace the origins of their faith back to a family member who was treated for Hansen's disease at Danja. Some have had prominent leadership positions in the church, in educational institutions, and in government.[71]

Malam Langa-Langa and the All-Meal Cookies

Elvin and Lolita Harbottle started the SIM work in Madaoua in 1951, and they lived there until their retirement in 1985, 34 years later. They did a lot of what was then called trekking—traveling around to villages in the surrounding area (sometimes on a motorcycle)—preaching and sharing the gospel. Chuck Truxton relates what they ate on those treks:

> Elvin had an ingenious solution for keeping the food supplies light and simple for the journey: before leaving home, he would cook up as many "all-meal" cookies as would be needed for the journey. By all accounts, the cookies were HUGE

---

[69] Ockers, "History of SIM Work in Niger," 35; Younge, "SIM in Niger," 55–56.
[70] World Health Organization, "Leprosy (Hansen's Disease)," 2023, https://www.who.int/data/gho/data/themes/topics/leprosy-hansens-disease.
[71] "Danja, An Eternal Healing Touch," *SIM NOW*, Winter 1994.

and packed with lots of wholesome ingredients. Breakfast, lunch and supper—the nutrition-packed cookies served to keep them going.[72]

Elvin earned the nickname Malam Langa-Langa for his resilience in the trekking ministry. A langa-langa is a light, hand-held scythe (sometime styled as a machete) used to cut one's way through the bush.

---

[72] Truxton, *The Quiet Passion Behind the Stones*, 65–66.

THE 1960s

The decade of the 1960s was a time of turmoil and change for the world. The Vietnam War left a legacy of pain and protest. There were social and political upheavals in many parts of the world, and the Iron Curtain separating communist eastern Europe from the representative democracies of Western Europe strengthened through the construction of the Berlin Wall in 1961. Assassinations of two key leaders in the US—John F Kennedy in 1963 and Martin Luther King, Jr. in 1968—brought national and international trauma. Before the end of the decade, on 20 July 1969, the world celebrated the first person to step on the moon. The Second Vatican Council (1962-1965) brought sweeping changes to the Catholic Church.

Newly independent African countries spread their wings and began the process of nation building. For Africa there was also a lot of upheaval and turmoil during the decade. Both the Democratic Republic of Congo and Nigeria experienced coups and conflict. For Nigeria, this meant civil war, testing whether the boundaries drawn by the colonial masters would survive or disappear. For Congo, there was the assassination of Patrice Lumumba and the installation of the brutal dictator Mobuto Sese Seko. Niger, for its part, gained full independence from France on 3 August 1960. It joined other African countries—32 in all—which became independent during the decade. The discovery of uranium in the Sahara in 1966 gave hope for a lucrative export that could help finance Niger's development.[73]

For SIM in Niger, there was less growth than in the 1950s, but two new ministry locations opened in the east. After a breakdown-plagued survey trip by Gordon Bishop, George Beacham, and David Knowlton in 1959, buildings were erected at two locations[74]: Maïné-Soroa (1961) and Gouré (1964).[75] The first missionaries in Maïné were George and Mae Beacham (1961-1964) and Chuck and Lois Forster (1961-1969). Carey and Shirley Lees started the work in Gouré and spent 27 years there (1964-1991). Jean Playfair, daughter-in-law of the previous general director of SIM, also spent 15 years in Gouré (1964-1979).

Tibiri School

One ministry that started in the 1960s was the primary school at Tibiri (1967). It was the brainchild of Gwen Van Lierop and was intended to give a Christian education to the children of Christians. Partly because of the previous tensions between the anglophone missionaries and the French administration, instruction was initially in English, but it was changed to French after two years.[76] This boarding school ministry went through quite a lot of turmoil and tension over the years and struggled to live up to its promise but had better success in later years.[77]

---

[73] "Uranium Find in Niger Republic," *Africa Now*, no. 35 (Oct-Dec) (1967): 13.
[74] Gordon Bishop, Gordon Beacham, and David Knowlton, "Pioneer Teams Survey Remote Tchad Basin," *Africa Now*, no. 5 (Apr-Jun) (1960): 6–8, 10–11.
[75] Ockers, "History of SIM Work in Niger," 55, 58.
[76] Nomaou and DeValve, Tsibiri dans les annees 1930-1970.
[77] Cooper, *Evangelical Christians in the Muslim Sahel*, 280–89; Ockers, "History of SIM Work in Niger—1923–2000," 21; Mahamane, "History and Challenges of the Evangelical Church in Niger, 1923–2013," 256, note 50.

Founding of the EERN

One of the most important events in Niger in the 1960s was the founding of a national church recognized by the independent government of Niger. The church needed to take on an authentic national image in front of the government in order to survive in the pressure of a heavily Islamic context. First, a committee was formed of Africans and missionaries to discuss and write the founding documents. This took several months to discuss and draw up, and there was considerable tension between SIM and the church over this process.[78] George Learned was heavily involved in this committee. The resulting constitution was signed by the church delegates and missionaries on 20 October 1960, and the Église Évangélique de la République du Niger—Evangelical Church of the Republic of Niger—(EERN) was formed. The government recognized the church on 31 January 1961.[79] The EERN has grown to include around 150 churches and over 8000 baptized members.[80]

Farm School at Maza Tsaye

John and Evelyn Ockers started a farm school for boys on the main road outside Maradi. John brought in farm implements (plows, tractors), used oxen to plow, started tree nurseries, and demonstrated how to get better crop yields from Niger's sandy soil. The school started off with 30 boys in 1958 at Maza Tsaye. Since they did not have permission to operate a school on the land, they plant-

---
[78] Dipple, "A Missiological Evaluation," 73–74.
[79] Ockers, "History of SIM Work in Niger," 21; Mahamane, "History and Challenges of the Evangelical Church in Niger, 1923–2013," 236–37.
[80] "Niger Church Statistics" (AMEEN, February 2017).

ed 25 acres of peanuts using his jeep station wagon as a tractor followed by the students using ox-drawn seeders. The peanuts grew so well they caught the attention of the local government officials and helped secure authorization to operate the school. Later, John was able to plant an experimental field of millet in which he showed how to increase the yield from 75 to 325 bundles per field, an astonishing 333%![81]

In addition to improved farming methods, the school also gave the students a thorough Bible education and six years of formal schooling in French. Although Barbara Cooper in her book critiques the farm school as contributing to land degradation and introducing unsustainable methods of farming,[82] the school was much appreciated by the government, and the effects of the school have lasted to the present day. Development work continues within the church and as an arm of SIM Niger. John's work and ministry continue at the site in Maza Tsaye, with its big, shady trees and its sweeping vistas of land which now includes a school and a conference center as well as being a base for Sowing Seeds of Change in the Sahel, with its experimental farms and tree nurseries. Gordon Evans, retired Maza Tsaye Conference Director, said that 'there is rarely a day goes by that I'm not reminded and impressed with the incredible foundations John and others laid here on this site'. John was awarded the Mérite Agricole du Niger by the government in 1968 for his work[83]. Due to the lack of a culturally acceptable way to integrate the students back into their communi-

---

[81] "Cultivating New Ideas in Niger," *Africa Now*, June 1978, 6.
[82] Cooper, *Evangelical Christians in the Muslim Sahel*, 273–79.
[83] "Obituary for John Ockers," January 5, 2017; Kerry Lovering, "Deep Roots," *Africa Now*, no. 18 (Jul-Sep) (1963): 8–9; Ockers, "History of SIM Work in Niger," 46–49.

ties, the farm school closed in 1977, but its legacy lives on.

Philanthropy to Qur'anic Students

Chuck and Lois Forster discovered a unique way to handle the Qur'anic students who came begging for alms at their door in Maïné-Soroa each day. They arranged with the bean cake sellers to come to the house each day at the same time the Qur'anic students arrived. Each young man would receive two bean cakes in their bowl. At first, the young men stood in a line to receive their bean cakes. Then, some wily boys tried to hurry back to the end of the line to try for another two! So, the Forsters required them all to sit down in a line to get their two cakes![84]

Aguié Bible School

After the recognition of the EERN by the government, the church decided to close the Bible school in Tibiri and find a more suitable place where the students could have land to farm. After some searching, a committee of missionaries and Nigeriens found a good site in Aguié, and the school was opened in 1964. David and Hazel (Nikki) Knowlton served as the first teachers with two couples and two single students in attendance. The missionary couple most associated with the school are George and Millie Learned, who taught there from 1965 until their retirement in 1991. Other missionaries who spent more than one year in Aguié were Jeanne Scypinski (1987-1993), Phyllis Erickson (1987-2005), and Martin & Lucie Brown (1989-1994). Today the school is entirely in the hands of the church. Until the time

---

[84] Ockers, "History of SIM Work in Niger," 57.

of writing, instruction has been in Hausa. All the teaching and administration is done by Hausa speakers.[85]

Decoration of SIM Missionaries (1964)

Several missionaries were decorated by the new Niger government during the 1960s. The first was Newton Kapp, superintendent of SIM work in Francophone. He received the *Chevalier de l'Ordre* award directly from the president, His Excellency Diori Hamani, in a ceremony in his honor held in Maradi on 10 June 1964. Others included several medical people. Dr. Burt Long, the founding doctor at Galmi Hospital, was one. He was not in Niamey for the presentation ceremony, but he received the *Chevalier de l'Ordre* from President Diori Hamani on 19 December 1964 for his services rendered to the country. On the same day three nurses also received awards for their services One of them was Genevieve Kooy, but much research has not revealed the names of the other two.[86]

Maternity Clinic in Guéchémé

Liz Chisolm trained as a nurse and arrived in Niger in 1953. For some ten years, she worked at the dispensary in Tibiri. Her work largely involved general medical work, treating infectious diseases, eye problems, and accident wounds. Comparatively little was done to care for women in pregnancy and labor and for infant and child

---

[85] Ibid., Ockers, 23–24; "Farmer Evangelistis Graduate in Niger," *Africa Now*, 1968.
[86] Long, A Family Living under the Sahara Sun, 274, 371; Cooper, Evangelical Christians in the Muslim Sahel, 295–96; Harold Fuller, Run While the Sun Is Hot (New York: Sudan Interior Mission, 1967); Ockers, "History of SIM Work in Niger," 22; Lovering, "Man with the Big Back Yard," 3.

care. Sensing the need for maternity and pediatric care, she trained as a midwife and was then transferred to Guéchémé, where in 1964, SIM opened a maternity clinic. Liz served ably there for over twelve years and gained quite a reputation. Women in the local population generally gave birth at home without the aid of midwives, birth attendants, or medical professionals. Only if they were in labor for days or had severe complications would they seek medical help. Thus, it was often the most complicated cases that appeared at the maternity. In such circumstances, it was not possible to save all the babies or mothers, but some lived, and women began coming from the surrounding region and from Nigeria to have their babies in Guéchémé. Unfortunately, the lack of staff and the responsibilities of running both a maternity and a general clinic as well as the relief work related to the great Sahel drought of the 1970s made it difficult to continue the medical work. It was simply unsustainable, and in 1976 the Guéchémé compound was handed over to the government. Liz Chisolm used her incredible skills as a nurse and administrator at Galmi Hospital for the rest of her career until she retired in the mid-1980s.[87]

Congo Nurse Serves at Galmi

Margaret Hayes served in the Democratic Republic of Congo during the early 1960s when the country gained its independence and suffered through severe upheaval and much violence at the hand of rebels and dictators.

---

[87] Barbara M Cooper, "Maternal Health in Niger and the Evangelical Imperative: The Life of a Missionary Nurse in the Post-War Era," in *Transforming Africa's Religious Landscapes: The Sudan Interior Mission (SIM), Past and Present* (Trenton, New Jersey: Africa World Press, 2018), 287–312; Elizabeth Chisolm, "Lessons from Liz Chisolm" (Charlotte, NC: SIM USA, 1988).

During the Simba rebellion in 1964, many foreigners, including quite a number of missionaries, were killed. She was saved from the massacre of 13 colleagues in one place by a local Christian who hid her in the jungle. When the outside world heard of the massacre, she was presumed dead, so no one tried to rescue her. In hiding she learned that the Simbas were searching for her, and that Christians were suffering reprisals for hiding her, so she resolved to give herself up and suffer a martyr's death. Instead, the Simbas needed a medically trained person and used her as a doctor for their warriors. She suffered incredible privations and some miraculous escapes from death in her 11 months in captivity. Finally, she came to the attention of the outside world, and mercenary soldiers freed her in a dramatic rescue. Her story is told in the book *Missing: Believed Killed* (1966). After her release, she could not return to the Congo immediately and applied with SIM to serve at Galmi. She worked there for a year before returning to the Congo in 1969. In the 1980s, she returned to Niger and ended her career with nine years at Galmi.[88]

Early Technology

In the early decades of SIM work in Niger, electric power was limited, and technology was primitive. One effective method of gospel proclamation was showing filmstrips using a gasoline generator to power the projector and sound. Missionaries would often stage showings of Bible stories and *Jungle Doctor* filmstrips dubbed into Hausa. This method was used to great effect in both Maïné-Soroa

---

[88] "Congo Nurse Now Serving in Niger," *Africa Now*, (May-Jun) (1968); Long, *A Family Living under the Sahara Sun*, 370.

and Tahoua in the 1960s. Hundreds of people showed up each night. One favorite filmstrip was entitled in Hausa 'Biri Mai Taurin Kai' (The Bull-Headed Monkey) and produced a lot of hilarity over the stubborn monkey who experienced calamity because he would not learn from his mistakes. The *Jungle Doctor* stories, authored by missionary doctor Paul White from Australia, were popular in mission circles in the 1950s and 1960s.[89]

Death of Evelyn Ockers

John and Evelyn Ockers went to Niger in 1949. Their ministry involved medical work, itinerant preaching, trekking, and church planting as well as the farm school. Evelyn was never in the best of health and struggled with the extreme climate. She was unable to perspire normally and constantly ran a low-grade fever. She required SIMAIR evacuation from the hot season in Niger to the more moderate climate of the plateau in central Nigeria two out of every three years in Niger. In April 1966, the Ockers were on their annual leave in Miango, Nigeria. Evelyn was not well, and even the cooler climate of the plateau did not seem to help. John returned to Maradi while Evelyn stayed for a medical checkup. She went into the hospital in May for tests, which revealed she had viral hepatitis. Her liver deteriorated quickly, and she fell into a hepatic coma. Early on 16 May 1966, she died. She is buried in the cemetery behind Kirk Chapel at Miango Rest Home.[90]

---

[89] "Filmstrips Captivate Niger Muslims," *Africa Now*, no. 46 (Sep-Oct) (1969): 14; Ockers, "History of SIM Work in Niger," 19, 58.
[90] "Obituary for John Ockers," 2; Truxton, *The Quiet Passion Behind the Stones*, 111–13.

Visit of Niger President to SIM HQ in Toronto

During the 1960s, SIM and the Evangelical Baptist Mission (EBM) enjoyed exceptionally good relations with the Niger government. Newton Kapp, district superintendent for SIM work in Francophone Africa, had a warm relationship with His Excellency Diori Hamani, the president of Niger.[91] In September 1969, Mr. Diori paid a 10-day visit to Canada. In Toronto, he visited SIM Canada Headquarters and invested SIM's General Director, Dr. Ray Davis, with the National Order of the Republic of Niger in recognition of SIM's contribution to the health and well-being of Niger. He praised SIM's work in the country and thanked Dr. Davis for the 'very significant' help afforded the nation.[92]

'Sai Galmi'

During his visit to the SIM Headquarters in Canada, His Excellency the President of Niger Diori Hamani gave a speech. Ruth Long in her book, *A Family Living Under the Sahara Sun*, reports what he said about Galmi:

> A hospital located in the town of Galmi has acquired a reputation for taking seemingly hopeless cases and restoring them to health. If some illness or accident seems nearly incurable, [local] people say, 'Sai Galmi' (Literally, 'Only Galmi,' meaning 'Only Galmi can help'). The expression has become part of popular speech, and now if a car is badly wrecked, its extreme condition is 'Sai Galmi.' [93]

---

[91] Lovering, "Man with the Big Back Yard," 2–3.
[92] Kerry Lovering, "Niger President Decorates Mission Leader," *Africa Now*, December 1969, 14; Long, *A Family Living under the Sahara Sun*, 370–71.
[93] Long, *A Family Living under the Sahara Sun*, 370; Harold Paul Adolph,

John Ockers expands on the meaning of the expression. Narrowly, it means that if a patient cannot find healing anywhere else or if his case is hopeless, he should try Galmi. More broadly, the expression is used to describe anything that is hopeless or beyond repair.[94] The story illustrates how a new expression entered the Hausa language, reinforcing the reputation of Galmi Hospital and spreading its renown to the ends of the earth. Of course, Galmi does not treat only the most extreme cases of injury and illness, but the name of the hospital is such that if you mention it anywhere in the country, people will often recognize it and know it by reputation if not by experience.

Fire at Galmi

One more story from Galmi. This one comes to us again from Ruth Long: It was the afternoon of March 12, 1969. Clap, clap, clap—the usual Hausa greeting at the door. The man seemed desperate and was breathing hard. Burt was asleep, and Ruth tried to ignore the greeting. But he was insistent. Clap, clap, clap, clap, clap. Then the visitor shouted 'Fire!' Burt woke up and quickly dashed off. Ruth followed, half walking, half running. Here is what she said about the sight she saw:

> I turned into the main entrance and saw men and women with their loads on their heads coming toward me. I saw men sliding along on the floor toward the exit with their legs in casts. There was a general exodus from the men's ward, adjacent to

---

Today's Decisions, Tomorrow's Destiny, (Spooner, WI: White Birch Printing, 1999), 156; "Sai Galmi," SIM NOW, 1993.
[94] Ockers, "History of SIM Work in Niger," 35.

the surgical wing. Smoke was pouring out of the surgical wing doors, but ... the fire was out. There were Burt and Ray (Pollen) and Dari and Boube and Mamman and Issa standing in water an inch deep, surrounded by buckets, some empty, some full of water. It wasn't the operating room, but the scrub room right next to it.... A 20-quart pressure cooker was standing on the two burner kerosene stove, filled with wrapped instruments, but still standing. Two tables were charred—only a few minutes before they had been ablaze, set on fire by the kerosene tank that fell from the stove after the soldering job had melted because of the intense heat. Boube had been sterilizing the instruments, had a good hot fire under the pressure cooker, so hot in fact that the soldered repair job wasn't adequate. When the tank fell and spilled, fire raced across the tables, aided by the spilled kerosene. Boube grabbed for a bucket, filled it with water, threw it on, but it did no good. He ran for the house and roused [others from their naps]. The African workers soon appeared out of the blue and the bucket brigade commenced. [Fortunately], no one was hurt.... The patients made their way back to their beds. The people were joyous and said 'Gaisheku', [which] meant, 'You did a great thing getting that fire out so quickly.'[95]

Electric Power in Galmi

One final story about Galmi for this chapter. In addition to all the continuing problems with water, doctors and residents had no electricity in the hospital and in their homes for the first fifteen years of the hospital's

---

[95] Long, *A Family Living under the Sahara Sun*, 316–17.

existence. At night, missionaries used kerosene lamps and flashlights at home, when out walking, or doing surgery in the hospital. During the hot season, surgery was a sweaty mess in scrubs and gloves with no fans or air conditioners. Often, a young man would fan the surgeon to keep his head free of perspiration. Still, according to Jim VerLee, a doctor at Galmi in the 1960s, 'glasses [got] steamed up, eyes fill[ed] with sweat, and sweat [ran] off elbows ... steadily.' [96] Slowly, funds were collected to buy a generator and build a house for a power plant. Finally, in May 1965, Wilf Husband and his helpers installed an 8.5 kw generator in the house built for it. They had to drag it nearly 200 meters with a Jeep, then roll it on pipes through the door, and finally put it into place. At first, electricity was only used to power fans and lights in surgery, then in the hospital wards. Then a year later, the houses on the compound got electricity. Here is how Jim VerLee tells the story:

> The biggest news item from Galmi hospital lately is the final completion of the electric wiring of the houses and regular operation of the electric plant for the hospital and houses at night. This has been years in preparation and is an example of the ponderous slowness of getting things accomplished [here]. We have had intermittent electric power in the hospital for use during surgery for a couple years, but now we have it in the houses too. No more lamp cleaning and lighting lamps each evening, and no more kicking around in dark rooms. We can use tape recorders and appliances. The convenience is wonderful![97]

---

[96] Jim VerLee, "VerLee Letters," 14 May 1963.
[97] VerLee, July 1966.

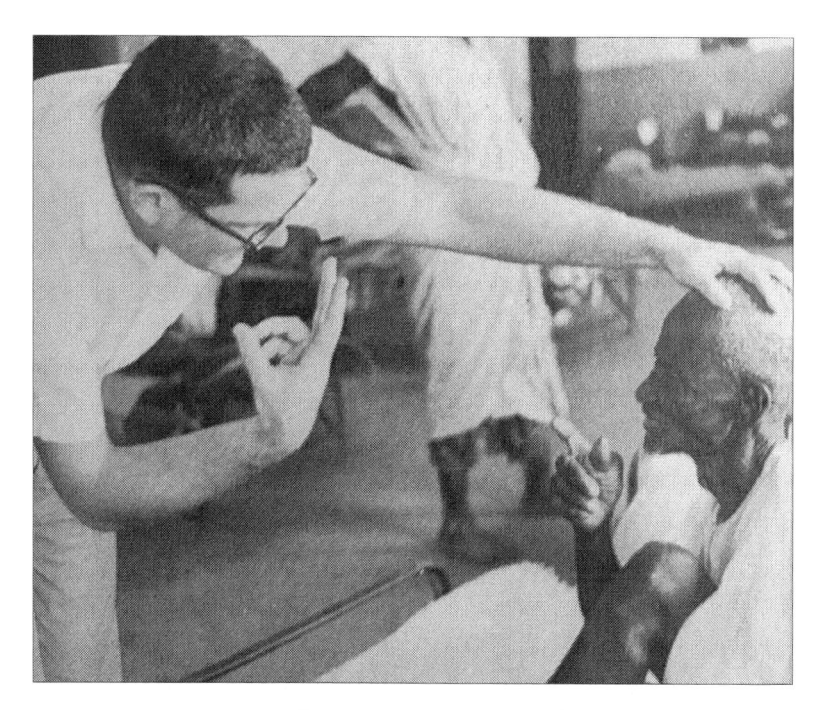

Jim VerLee was one of two surgeons at Galmi Hospital during the 1960s. Galmi averaged about 200 operations monthly. Here Dr. VerLee tests the sight of a ptient after corrective surgery. The fine Sahara dust accounts for Niger's high incidence of eye disorders.

THE 1970s

The decade of the 1970s was a time of economic and political upheaval and uncertainty. The hijacking and spectacular destruction of several planes by Palestinian militants at the beginning of the decade shocked the world. There was a surge in terrorism with the abduction and subsequent death of 11 Israeli hostages at the 1972 Olympics and the hijacking of a Lufthansa flight later that year. At the end of the decade, the Iranian Revolution precipitated the storming of the US Embassy in Iran and the holding of 52 American hostages, a crisis that lasted 444 days. Wars hot and cold flared throughout the 1970s. The Vietnam War ended with the Communist north taking over the south and a time of defeat and soul-searching for the United States. Later in the decade, the Soviet Union invaded Afghanistan (1979) and got bogged down in guerilla warfare. On the hopeful side, Israel and Egypt signed a historic peace treaty in Washington in March 1979 after the Camp David Accords.

The decade also witnessed the Arab oil embargo (1973), when countries in the Middle East asserted their new-found oil wealth and political muscle and triggered a recession in the US and Europe by stopping oil shipments to Western countries. The resulting shortages created long lines at petrol pumps, and price increases in the cost of petrol spurred massive inflation. In 1975, prices rose 25% in the UK, for example.[98]

---

[98] Sarah Janssen, ed., *The World Almanac and Book of Facts, 2022* (New York, NY: World Almanac Books, 2022), 668.

In Africa, the last remaining countries still under European domination gained independence from colonial powers. Most of these were former Portuguese colonies (Cabo Verde, Guinea-Bissau, São Tomé and Principe, Angola, and Mozambique), but there were also two island countries in the Indian Ocean (Comoros and Seychelles) as well as Western Sahara and Djibouti. South Africa was still ruled by a white minority government which tried to entrench apartheid in its social and political infrastructure, but all other countries were ruled by their own people. Zimbabwe was not to gain final independence until 1980, but it already was under majority rule by 1979.

For Niger, the decade of the 1970s was a difficult time. The Sahel drought of 1973-1975 resulted in many deaths and widespread hunger.[99] The handling of the drought and the accusations of widespread corruption were factors in the downfall of the Diori government on 15 April 1974. President Diori's wife lost her life in the coup[100]. Lieutenant-Colonel Seyni Kountché became president of a military government that lasted until 1993, when elections were held for the third republic.

SIM Niger saw many changes during the decade. SIM administration for the three French-speaking countries where SIM worked (Niger, Dahomey, and Upper Volta) was moved from Maradi to Niamey in 1972 and detached from SIM headquarters in Jos, Nigeria. A new Francophone administrative office was set up in Niamey to care for arriving missionaries with Howard Dowdell as the first area director. In 1974, the Ecole Biblique (Bible School) opened. It had previously been set up in Mahadaga, Upper Volta, but that was a rural area where French was

---

[99] "Famine," *Africa Now* Sept-Oct, no. 70 (1973): 8–9.
[100] "Niger: SIM OK after Coup," *Africa Now* Jul-Aug, no. 75 (1974): 11.

not as commonly spoken. It was moved to Niamey to train pastors and leaders from all three French-speaking countries.[101] In addition, the 1974 coup changed relationships between SIM and the Niger government. While there were still good relationships, the contacts changed from informal and cordial to more formal and official. The decade also saw an expansion of SIM ministries to encompass the eastern Fulani with Pat and Juanita Paternoster and Phil and Carol Short.

SIM Niger's Work in the East

Many SIM Niger missionaries served in difficult situations and places. Here is the story of one couple, Pat and Juanita Paternoster. Pat was born in the UK, and Juanita came from the US. Pat went to Nigeria in 1951 to work as an accountant, and there he became a follower of Christ and met Juanita, who worked with the Nigerian Faith Mission. After their marriage in 1956, they were accepted with SIM and spent most of the 1960s working in different administrative capacities in Nigeria.

Attracted by the work among nomads from the Sahel, they requested a transfer to Zinder for their third term. For the next 19 years (1971-1990), they concentrated on trekking in the Zinder/Tanout area, sharing the good news amongst nomads around wells and encampments. At the same time, they raised six children in a tiny house converted from a church into a dwelling.

The work of the Paternosters was discouraging and tiring, and they had to retire in 1992 after being medically evacuated from Niger. It was a great encouragement to

---

[101] "Niamey Bible School," 1980, SIM Int'l.

them when their son Dan returned to Niger in 1993 and saw God do an amazing work among the nomads, reaping the first fruits of the harvest his parents had sown.[102]

'Come ... but Live Among My People!'

The following is not so much a story as a reflection on SIM's work in Niger in the early 1970s. It is an excerpt from *Africa Now,* an exhortation to SIM missionaries written by Mr. Oumarou Youssoufou, the first secretary of the Niger Embassy in Washington. While it serves as a critique of SIM in Niger, it also illustrates the deep relationship between SIM and the Nigerien government at the time.

> I am for sending more missionaries to evangelize, but I am in total disagreement with the present system.
>
> I have observed missionaries and Peace Corps volunteers in Africa in the past ten years, and, in spite of some criticisms, my very sincere admiration goes to the Peace Corps. There are few missionaries who compare favorably with the Peace Corps volunteers, but, in general, I have found more understanding of our traditional African life among volunteers than among missionaries. As far as language is concerned, there, too, the Peace Corps volunteers are far ahead ... [One] Peace Corps volunteer ... after three years in Niger was more fluent in Hausa than any missionary ... and some have been there close to forty years. The Peace Corps volunteers live among the people, eat the

---

[102] Howard E Brant, "Niger—Land of Standing Millet Stalks: A Report on SIM's Ministry in Niger, West Africa" (Charlotte, NC: SIM International, June 13, 1988), 22–23; Dan Paternoster, "Report of October 1993 Mission," February 20, 1994.

same food as the people, sleep in the same type of huts without running water or electricity.

Missionaries seem to insist that they cannot live in our "dirty, primitive villages, because they may get some of our multiple diseases." Only a handful can claim having ever tasted our foods.

Yes, I sound negative about what missionaries are doing. I sound negative because I am concerned. I sound negative because there have been missionaries like SIM's ... Dr. Andrew Stirrett, known in Jos as "Bature Mai-Magani" (the white man with medicine), [who] spent more time in Jos market and among Nigerians than in the secluded Jos mission compound.

I know of no Muslim head of state who has been as kind to missionaries as my President, His Excellency Diori Hamani ... [He] has said over and over again that he admires missionaries, that he has seen the many establishments they have in other African countries, and he wants the same establishments in Niger.

As a government employee and as a Christian, I urge those Christians of good will who are able to accept an uneducated and poor Fulani as his equal to come to Niger with something to offer us. I insist on this because I have noticed that it is easier for some missionaries to accept the so called "sophisticated" people as equals and consider their cooks and boys as inferiors. I find it hard to believe that you can lead anyone to the Lord if you insist on maintaining a master-servant relationship.[103]

---

[103] Oumarou Youssoufou, "Come ... But Live Among My People," *Africa Now*, no. 60 (February 1972): 6.

A hard-hitting—perhaps controversial—message, but one that still provokes thought and reflection. Bruce Dipple, who lectured at the Niamey Bible School in Niamey from 1976 to 1984, states further that early missionaries were more concerned with evangelism than with learning about the people and culture and made many mistakes as a result.[104]

A New SIMAIR Base in Niger

Up until the 1970s the SIMAIR base for West Africa was in Jos, Nigeria. With the opening of the new Francophone administration office and with the need for a flight program which did not necessitate filing permissions to cross into French countries, a new base for SIMAIR operations was established in Niamey in September 1973. Jim Rendel was the first pilot/mechanic, and Bob Forward joined him a year later. A Christian businessman/builder, upon learning that SIMAIR had no hangar, financed and built one for SIM. It was completed in 1975.

Another project was the construction of the airstrip in Galmi in late 1974, with the first flight into Galmi early in 1975. Ruth Long takes up the story:

> An Aztec, 6-passenger, 2 motor plane circled the station and finally settled down on the end of the airstrip, coming to a halt ¾ of the way down the strip. Accompanied by Bob Forward, three French aeronautical inspectors came to inspect our finished airstrip. After months of negotiations with the farmers from whom we wanted to buy some land and the road paving company who agreed to do the work, finally the all-weather laterite topped

---

[104] Dipple, "A Missiological Evaluation," 94–96.

A dust storm forms over the SIMAIR hangar in 2014.

airstrip was completed ... And who else was there? The whole town, of course. It was like market day. At least a thousand people came running from every direction to see this "big bird come down out of the sky" and land in our backyard. No more running back and forth to the airstrip in Malbaza, 14 miles away. No more waiting for planes scheduled to come but delayed along the way. No more wasting the pilot's time after he buzzed our station, giving us the signal to meet the plane ... No more transporting ill or wounded patients to the other airstrip ... Would the inspectors approve? After parking the plane, they rode down to the end of the strip west in the V.W. Bug, then back up to the east end behind the hospital, and after a cup of coffee ... they gave their approval. Permission was granted just in time, for within a half hour we were expecting a plane of our own to buzz us with two passengers ... So when the [second] plane buzzed us ... we gave him the signal to come on in. Thus, on Jan. 20, 1975, our little airstrip was inaugurated.[105]

SIMAIR has flown thousands of passengers and gone many hundreds of thousands of miles since its base in Niger was established. In all that time there have been several mishaps, including one in June 1975 where a plane went off the end of the Galmi strip due to a brake failure, but there has never been a fatal accident.

The Drought of the 1970s

The first half of the decade was a period of drought and hunger for Niger. Official rainfall statistics for Niamey show that rainfall was below average every year from 1970 to 1974 except in 1971. Average rainfall in the twentieth century was around 572 mm (22.5 in). In 1973, only 370 mm (14.6 in) of rain fell in the entire rainy season[106]. Crops failed and as many as 80% of the cattle in the country died or were driven south to Nigeria. Many of the semi-nomadic peoples of Niger lost their livelihoods and were driven into cities to seek help and find work. SIM missionaries and the EERN did everything they could to alleviate the situation and provide relief. Some established food distribution programs with money. Others operated food-for-work programs. Rural development programs dug wells, planted trees, and promoted irrigation and water conservation. Galmi Hospital operated a program to provide food and medical care for vulnerable children. SIM missionaries col-

---
[105] Long, *A Family Living under the Sahara Sun*, 441–42.
[106] M V K Sivakumar, *Le Climat de Niamey* (Niamey, NIGER: Centre Shélien de l'ICRISAT, 1986), 7.

lected US$1,000—nearly US$7,000 in 2023 dollars—and contributed the funds to the government relief program. One remarkable story from this time concerns the transport of relief supplies to needy people. A heavy-duty vehicle was needed to insure the movement of grain and food products from purchase site to distribution centers. A Lebanese pilot on holiday had crossed the Sahara on a truck with his family. Traveling through Agadez, he was converted by Baptist missionaries. When he arrived in Niamey, he repurposed the truck and worked with SIM in distributing food aid. When he left, several Nigerien businessmen, impressed with the distribution program, pitched in to buy the truck so it could continue to be used for the relief project.[107]

Death of Deputy Director

Roland J. Pickering had worked in Dahomey among the Dompago people and had translated the New Testament into their language. He became deputy director for the new Francophone area of SIM when Howard Dowdell was director. Before any handover could officially occur, he died in a vehicle accident just outside Niamey on 5 October 1974 while returning to Niamey from Dahomey. The other occupants of the car, Madougou Ourou, Pat Burns, and JoAnn Franz, were all seriously injured, but Roland was thrown out of the vehicle through the window and died instantly. It was a big blow for SIM Niger to lose such a promising and capable leader.[108]

---

[107] "SIM Helps Famine Victims in East and West Africa," *Africa Now* Nov-Dec (1973): 9–10; "Drought Damage W. Africa Worsens," *Africa Now* Jul-Aug (1974): 10–11.

[108] Kerry Lovering, ed., "Missionary Dies in Crash," *Africa Now*, Nov-Dec (1974): 11; Howard Dowdell, "Death of Roland Pickering," Letter, October 11, 1974, SIM Int'l.

You Bought It, You Wear It

Phil and Carol Short first went to Niger in 1974 and have been committed to sharing the good news with people in the east of the country for over fifty years, which is half of the time that this book commemorates. The following story comes from their early years of ministry in Maïné-Soroa.

During their first term of four years in the country, they were often discouraged. They felt like they could have packed up and gone home. Phil used to lie in bed and study the corrugated metal ceiling. There were 48 corrugations, the same number of the months in their term of service. Phil would count down those corrugations month by month, wondering how he could possibly last that long until their return to Australia.

One of the things that helped break the ice in their work was when Phil asked the local people what they thought of the way he dressed. Up to that point, he had worn a shirt tucked into his trousers and a floppy hat like he wore in Australia. After some hesitation and a bit of doubtful encouragement from Phil, they replied, 'Well, you're supposed to be a full-grown man and a religious teacher, but you dress like a little boy.'

That did it. Phil went to the market and bought cloth and had a tailor make it into a long gown with matching baggy trousers. He also bought a hat that was more appropriate for the context. After trying on the new outfit, he looked at himself in the mirror. He felt rather embarrassed and silly and asked Carol, 'What do you think?' She said, 'You bought it; you wear it.'

There was no backing down now. Cautiously, Phil made his way into the market to greet and speak to people. Nobody laughed or looked askance at him. Instead, he received many compliments. 'Now you look like a teacher,' they said. After that nobody asked what kind of work Phil was doing. They knew what he did from the clothes he wore[109].

God at Work through the Danja Leprosarium

One family experienced the goodness of God at the leprosarium in Danja in the 1970s. The patriarch of the family was a marabout who taught Arabic in Madaoua. One of the man's four wives contracted leprosy, and the family was desperate to find a treatment, visiting all kinds of Muslim and traditional healers to find a cure. After much searching the family heard about the leprosarium and sent the woman and her four children to Danja, where they were greeted by Virginia Fridal, director of the leprosarium at the time. During the six months of treatment, the woman and her children heard the good news for the first time. The three older children gave their lives to Christ, but the younger, a boy named Moussa Djibo, returned to Madaoua with his mother and began Qur'anic school. When he learned that his playmates were going off to government school, he wanted to go as well. He became the only member of his family who went to formal school. For a while, he wavered between the Christian faith and Islam, but he decided to follow Christ in 1985 when he was in junior high school. After he asked God to show him the truth, he had a dream in which Jesus took him in his arms, and from then on, he became a follower of Jesus. He studied at the teacher training college in Dosso and was

---

[109] Kerry Lovering, "You Bought It, You Wear It," *SIM NOW*, 1986, 2–3.

assigned to the Téra region as a primary school teacher. Later, he taught in the Mayahi area, where he met a missionary from Calvary Ministries. Sensing a call from God, he moved with his family to Nigeria for training and then joined Calvary Ministries as their first Nigerien missionary. In 2023, Moussa and his wife Marthe became the directors of Calvary Ministries (CAPRO) in Niger. They have six children, all grown, and live in Niamey[110]. As for Virginia Fridal, she received a medal of honor from the Niger government for her distinguished service at Danja before her retirement in 2000.[111]

The Mystery of the Stolen Money

Leonardo Navarra was a SIM missionary from Italy who, before becoming a believer, had been his father's secretary in the Mafia. After coming to Christ, he went to Niger and had an amazing ministry with youth in Zinder from 1974 until his untimely death in 1990. His Hausa name was Malam Murna (Mister Joy). He would show silent Charlie Chaplin movies to over 200 young people every night. In the middle of the movie, he would stop the film and have a local believer give a brief message. Then he would conclude the movie.

When Leonardo's father died, he received a small fortune in $100 American bills and Italian money. He stored this money in a safe in his house. One Sunday, while he was at church, thieves broke in and stole all the money from the safe. Influenced by his mafia days, Leonardo had copied down the serial numbers of all the bills. He went

---

[110] Moussa Djibo, "Moussa Djibo Testimony," March 3, 2023.
[111] Ockers, "History of SIM Work in Niger—1923–2000," 36.

to the local bank and requested that if anyone tried to cash in a $100 bill, they should call him immediately. Sure enough, a short time later, the bank called saying someone had just presented a $100 bill to exchange it for local money. Leonardo hurried to the bank, presented his list of serial numbers, and verified that the number on the bill matched one of the numbers on his list. The thieves turned out to be boys in Leonardo's youth group. All the stolen money was recovered, and Leonardo recommended the boys be reprimanded severely and let go on probation.[112]

First SIM Missionaries from Asia

In the decade of the 1970s SIM accepted its first missionaries from Asia. Dr. Andrew and Belinda Ng, who hail from Singapore, chose to serve at Galmi Hospital, where Andrew was a surgeon for 11 years beginning in 1979. They were trailblazers, opening the way for many more missionaries from the most populous continent. After they left Niger, Andrew became East Asia Office Sending Director and later Deputy International Director of SIM for East Asia and served in those roles for many years, greatly expanding the work of SIM in Singapore and throughout Asia.

First EERN Church in Niamey

The church had drawn up plans. A request had been submitted to the relevant government office some time before. Christians had been praying, both in Niger and elsewhere. But still permission had not been granted by the authorities to build a church in Niamey. This would be the

---
[112] Ibid., 10–11.

first Hausa church in the capital, but the response had not yet come. At a prayer meeting late in 1978, one Hausa church leader excitedly entered the building holding up a sheaf of papers in his hand for all to see. 'Look', he said, 'here is the final permission to begin building our church—all signed and sealed!'. That prayer meeting turned into a praise meeting. That church became the Hausa church in the Boukoki neighborhood.[113]

---

[113] George and Mae Beacham, "How God Answered Your Prayers: Niamey, Niger Republic," *Africa Now*, 1978, 8, SIM Int'l.

THE 1980s

The 1980s was a time of hope and euphoria. After a serious recession at the beginning of the decade, economic and social expectations recovered and remained high. It seemed like the world was on course for an unprecedented time of peace and prosperity. New gadgets like personal computers, VCRs, and video games began to appear on markets. The two great superpowers—the Soviet Union and the US—pursued policies of détente and *glasnost* (openness) as relations eased and disarmament ensued. The decade saw the end of the Cold War and the fall of the Berlin Wall after Ronald Reagan famously challenged the Soviet leader, 'Mr. Gorbachev, tear down this wall.' Not all was benign and peaceful, however. There was repression and reactionary movements in several countries—notably in Iran with the Islamic Revolution (1978-1981) and in China with Tiananmen Square (June 1989). Terrorism was on the rise, and three world leaders were assassinated during the decade: Anwar al-Sadat of Egypt (1981), Indira Gandhi of India (1984), and Rashid Karami of Lebanon (1987).

In Africa there was a massive drought in 1981-1985 that left nearly one-third of the population facing prolonged hunger and malnutrition, particularly in the Sahel and in Ethiopia. Live Aid, a marathon rock concert held simultaneously in both the UK and the USA in July 1985, raised relief funds but fueled misunderstanding about and paternalism toward Africa. In South Africa, the apartheid regime was faltering with economic sanctions imposed by the rest of the world and unrest within the country. In 1988, the country agreed to withdraw its occupying forces, present since World War II, from Southwest Africa. The new country, now named Namibia, gained its independence on 21 March 1990.

The 1980s were a time of great hunger and mourning for the country of Niger. The drought that affected the rest of the Sahel in 1983-85 had a profound impact on Niger. In 1987, the president of Niger, his Excellency Seyni Kountché, died of a brain tumor, and the country went into a period of mourning and upheaval in the transition to democracy. There were demonstrations and protests against the government and its policies, notably a protest on the Kennedy Bridge over the Niger River on 9 February 1990 in which some students died.[114]

This decade saw an expansion of the work of SIM in the Maradi area, particularly amongst the Fulani and in the realm of agriculture. It also saw the establishment of Sahel Academy in Niamey in 1986. The Niamey Office moved from the downtown area to its current location just off Tillabéri Road in 1985. During the decade, there were also SIM missionaries stationed in Diffa—Lorna Downes and Cathy Jones, the famous Dow/Jones duo.

Farmer-Managed Natural Regeneration (FMNR)

Tony Rinaudo and his wife Liz were SIM Niger missionaries from 1980 to 1999. An agriculturalist by training, Tony hails from Australia. While in Niger, he pioneered a technique for reforestation of degraded land called FMNR. Here is his story of how he discovered this technique:

---

[114] Mahamane, "History and Challenges of the Evangelical Church in Niger, 1923–2013," 244.

In 1983, after two and a half years of mounting frustration at both tree planting and at gaining popular community acceptance for this activity, I was ready to give up. On a particularly low day as I was driving to the villages with a trailer load of seedlings, the hopelessness of it all weighed heavily on me. Looking over the barren landscape one didn't have to be a rocket scientist to see that using these conventional reforestation approaches, I would never make a significant or lasting impact. I was considering giving up and going home. Even so, I still felt I was meant to be in Niger, and I prayed a simple prayer, asking God to forgive us for destroying the gift of his beautiful creation and for him to open my eyes and to show me what to do.

Standing there, a common small 'bush' growing in the field caught my eye. I had 'seen' these bushes many times before but had not given them any thought—they appeared to be weeds, or at best, desert bushes. I walked over to take a closer look but recognized the shape of the leaves and immediately realised that this was not a bush at all—it was a tree that had been cut down and was sprouting from the stump. That realization changed everything. I immediately knew that this was the solution I had been looking for—and it had been at my feet the whole time! Across this seemingly barren landscape were millions of similar bushes representing a vast underground forest. Each year sprouting stems grow to about one metre in height—and are then slashed by farmers preparing their land for sowing the crops. Branches and leaves were burnt for ash to fertilise the soil and stems were collected for firewood. This annual slashing and burning prohibited the bushes from regrowing into full sized trees. After felling a tree, much of the root mass remains alive and most species can regrow rapidly from the stump. Felled trees constitute underground forests—we do not see it and are often unaware of the enormous potential for seemingly insignificant bushes to become trees.

This 'discovery' was in fact a rediscovery of an ancient practice which for various reasons had fallen out of use, due to population pressure and modern farming ideas. This rediscovery changed everything: reforestation was no longer a question of having the right technology or enough funding, staff or time. Nor was it about fighting the Sahara Desert, or goats or drought. Because everything you need for reforestation is literally at your feet, the battle was now about challenging deeply held beliefs, attitudes and practices and convincing people that it would be in their best interests to allow at least some of these bushes to become trees again. Because it was peoples' actions which had reduced the forest to a barren landscape, it would require people to restore it. False beliefs, attitudes and practices would need to be challenged with truth, through love, by example and with perseverance. Starting with just a dozen farmers willing to try this new approach, the practice of managing the regrowth from tree stumps to grow into trees spread across 50% of the agricultural land of Niger in 20 years. Today it continues to spread globally as it becomes increasingly well-known and appreciated.[115]

---

[115] Tony Rinaudo, "The Discovery of FMNR," April 3, 2023; Dave Hooker, "The Aussie Forest Maker Helping to Heal the Planet," *Eternity*, November 5, 2021, https://www.eternitynews.com.au/world/the-aussie-forest-maker-helping-to-heal-the-planet/?fbclid=IwAR013490joI8NNVSH5KCohgybZIaEejuY-76oFKX4_WtUbiFHzow97t61GfE; Jayson Casper, "The Forest Underground:

Maradi, Niger, before and after FMNR. Left: Tony Rinaudo in the early 1980s with pick up and trailer load of trees destined for planting. Right: The same area that has now been regreened through FMNR, 2017. (© World Vision)

FMNR has become recognized internationally to restore and maintain deforested land, and where goes the forest, so goes the environment. After 20 years FMNR has spread to 5 million hectares (12.4 million acres) of farmland in Niger, an area almost the size of the island of Tasmania! This is equal to approximately 200 million trees. The most recent study estimates that FMNR is now practiced on over 6 million hectares of farmland in Niger. The technique is the subject of a 2022 book by Tony entitled *The Forest Underground: Hope for a Planet in Crisis.* Tony was awarded the commander of merit (Commandeur du Mérite, Agricole) for his agricultural work by the Niger government in 1999.

How An Australian Missionary Regrew the Sahel," *Christianity Today*, November 10, 2022, https://www.christianitytoday.com/news/2022/november/cop27-forest-underground-niger-trees-sim-creation-care-fmnr.html; Tony Rinaudo, "The Development of Farmer Managed Natural Regeneration," *Leisa Magazine* 23, no. 2 (June 2007): 32–34.

Nomads Encounter the Good News

During the great drought of 1983-1985, many nomadic Fulani lost all their animals and migrated south to the larger cities looking for work and sustenance. John Ockers relates what happened.

> One evening early in 1984, Gordon and Lena Bishop, who were then living at Soura, were interrupted by clapping at the door, the customary way of making one's presence known. Gordon went out and found a number of people on donkeys. After the usual greetings, he asked where they were going at that time of night. As they literally fell off their donkeys, exhausted and hungry after their 80-mile trek, they said, 'We have arrived!'
>
> That was the tip of the iceberg, for within six months, some 2,500 Fulanis were camped at Soura receiving food aid and learning gardening under a SIM supervised program, most for the very first time ... Pastor 'Dan Nana and members of his family helped minister to them.[116]

Many missionaries and Nigeriens were involved in helping these Fulani. Tony Rinaudo's team, led by Ibrahim Yahaya, showed them how to make dry season gardens as a food-for-work scheme. Gordon Bishop helped dig wells to provide them with water. But many died of diseases and malnutrition. At one point a measles epidemic swept through the camp, killing dozens of malnourished people in a week. During the time they were there, the missionaries distributed gospel cassettes in their language and portable players operated by turning a crank manually.

---

[116] Ockers, "History of SIM Work in Niger," 42–44.

These cassettes circulated amongst the people and were carried back north when the seasonal rains returned in 1985.

Later in 1985, two young nomadic Fulani men went to Maradi to look for a white person to help them. There they encountered SIM missionaries, Anne Locke and Rhoda Miller, who invited them in and talked with them for a long time. They were suspicious of the missionaries, having heard unsavory rumors about them, but they found the rumors to be unfounded. As they talked and listened, they were attracted to the faith of the missionaries. Phil Short was asked to come and speak to them as he knew their language. They received the good news with gladness.

After two months in Maradi, the two men returned to their family encampment. On arrival, they found N sitting by himself. Many nomadic Fulani believe that natural elements sometimes communicate messages. A few hours prior, N had heard two doves chattering above him in the trees, and he believed this to indicate that he would soon receive some very good news. He told his wives to prepare food for some visitors. When his two kinsmen arrived and told him that they were now following Jesus, he immediately chose to follow as well. (In fact, N had heard the good news ten years prior and desired to follow, but family pressure dissuaded him.) This is one story among many about the spread of the good news amongst the Fulani of central Niger.[117]

---

[117] T I, "Recollections of a Fulani," July 23, 2023; Ockers, "History of SIM Work in Niger," 44–45.

An Accidental Death

In SIM, we believe that God has rescued us from sin, death, punishment, and Satan through the death and resurrection of Jesus Christ. We are committed to sharing this good news with those who have not heard it. Past chapters have recounted the stories of some who gave their lives in that cause. Here is another from the 1980s.

Gordon Bishop had been with SIM in Niger almost 40 years, serving some of that time in leadership. He had already officially retired but returned to Niger in 1983 for one last term before finally retiring to Canada in 1985. On the morning of 23 October 1984, he was helping to dig a new well outside of Maradi during the great drought that year. The Fulani who had come south after losing their livelihoods—their animals—needed more water for survival. Many of the surrounding wells had already gone dry. That morning, before the arrival of the SIM Rural Development crew, he had set up a tripod of heavy steel I-beams over the well to lower the circular concrete liner sections into the pre-dug well. After the workers arrived, they started the process of lowering the first liner section into the well. Suddenly, the tripod collapsed. Weighted by the concrete liner, one leg of the tripod fell across Gordon's back, pinning him to the edge of the well. 'Get this weight off of me,' he whispered. He quickly lapsed into unconsciousness as the workers struggled to remove the I-beam from his body. He was rushed to the hospital in Maradi, but it was too late. He was gone. He died as he lived, committed to demonstrating God's love in practical ways and in verbal communication. He is buried at the SIM cemetery in Tibiri near Maradi. His wife Lena was handed a notebook from his pocket which contained the following entry for 19 October: 'Are you ready for the day when you will come before God?'[118]

Some of Gordon's last words come from a prayer letter he wrote on 17 October 1984, just days before his death. His heart's desire at the time of his death was to see disciples trained to obey everything Jesus taught. In the letter, he recognized some of the mistakes he and previous missionaries had made. Here is what he said:

> If I had been able to begin my work in Africa with the knowledge that I gained only six years ago, my whole missionary career would have been vastly more effective. My hindsight will not recover those lost years, but hopefully what I will say will help others to avoid the big mistake I made. Today discipleship has become a common expression to us, and yet, how many missionaries are actually practicing it? When I started at Zinder in 1944 the word was unheard of and has only been heard in recent years…. Discipleship is the heart of our work. Without it you have weak, untaught believers who will never do much for the Lord and there will be no Spirit-filled leaders. Leaders do not come naturally; they are made by mature Christians with a vision of spending time with key men.[119]

What a sobering critique from an exemplary missionary! A new Hausa songbook was dedicated to Gordon's memory. He had devoted a considerable amount of work and time in bringing the book to completion.

---
[118] Kerry Lovering, "Lena, It's About Gordon," *SIM NOW* Mar-Apr, no. 20 (1985): 5; Lena Bishop, "Gordon Bishop's Death," November 2, 1984; Swanson, Alan, "Death of Gordon Bishop," October 25, 1984.
[119] Steve Schmidt, "Reflections on the History of SIM in Niger" (Powerpoint, Orientation, Niamey, NIGER, October 2015).

Follow the Bouncing Tyre

John and Nancy DeValve traveled with Les Boyd from Galmi to Maradi in early June 1986. It was a Sunday and the feast day after Ramadan, so traffic was light. The rainy season had not yet started, so it was also extremely hot, and the car had no ac. John, Nancy, and Les left Galmi at 9:30 a.m., hoping to arrive in Maradi by lunchtime. About halfway between Galmi and Maradi, they were rolling merrily along at 100 km per hour when suddenly, as they rounded a curve, the car started wobbling and then listing to the left. At the same time, they spied something bouncing through the bush on their right. "What's that?" Nancy said. "It's our tire," Les shouted. The naked left rear brake drum then hit the ground, and the car skidded to the left with a loud, grating sound and stopped.

The edge of the road had been washed out, and the car was now perched on the edge of an asphalt incline. It was difficult to get the jack under the car because there was no shoulder. There was no rock in the area suitable to place the jack on, so they used an old jerry can. They tried to jack up the car, but the jack broke. What next? They hailed a car down and were able to borrow a jack to get a spare tire on (the car was equipped with three spare tires!). They had to borrow a lug from each of the other tires so each tire had only three lugs.

Back on the road, John, Nancy, and Les felt the tire still wobbling. Upon inspection, they realized that the lugs did not fit properly in the tire holes, and the tire could not be tightened properly. It was gradually jiggling the lugs off. They would have to change to another tire. Fortunately, they were then at a village. Since they had no jack, they wondered how they would raise the car. The villagers came to the rescue. About 20 of them lifted the car, dug a small hole in the sand under the tire, and positioned a pounding pot upside down under the car. Les released the spare that was under the car, but the tire holder would not go back up, and you could not go 100 km with it dragging on the ground. There was nothing available with which to tie it up. Finally, they found a piece of string attached to a tool in the car to secure it. After changing the tire, they were on their way, with the villagers again lifting the car to take out the pounding pot. They proceeded more slowly and arrived in Maradi only six hours after they left Galmi, dirty, tired, and sweaty.[120]

The Opening of Sahel Academy

Until the 1980s, many of SIM Niger's Missionary Kids (MKs) went to Nigeria for their school years, attending Kent Academy (which only offered grades 1 through 9) in Miango and then Hillcrest School in Jos for secondary school. During the 1980s, it became harder and harder to procure visas for children to enter Nigeria and clearances for SIMAIR to fly them there. Then in 1984 the border between the two countries suddenly closed after a coup. Not only did this cut off aid to Niger, but it meant that getting in and out of Niger was impossible by road[121]. Several missionaries from Niger were caught off guard while on holiday in Nigeria when this happened. They had to leave their vehicles in Nigeria and fly back to Niger. Later, the MKs who went to school in Nigeria

---
[120] John R DeValve, "Trip to Galmi" Journal 7 (June 12, 1986).
[121] Anthony Asiwaju, "Back Again at Draconian Border Closure Policy," *Punch*, August 29, 2019, https://punchng.com/back-again-at-draconic-border-closure-policy/.

had to be flown home for the holidays via Lomé, Togo on a commercial airliner.[122] This was unquestionably an expensive and inconvenient option. For these reasons, plans were drawn up to establish a school in Niamey. A suitable property was found next to the Ecole Biblique along the river in Haro Banda. A former tile factory, the existing three buildings were converted to classroom space, a library, and a small auditorium. The school opened its doors in September 1986, and Pat Irwin was the first principal. There were 18 students the first year in grades one through seven.[123]

Tell Everyone

The following is a story related by Bev Botheras, who spent many years in both Nigeria and Niger. It explains the reason SIM missionaries are in Niger and what motivates them.

> Alhaji came to Galmi Hospital for treatment for TB. He became very interested in the stories of Jesus as told by SIM missionary Esther Grant and would regularly call others to come listen with him when she arrived to teach them. He even inquired how he might receive this forgiveness that Jesus offers.
>
> After a time, he returned to his home village some distance away. He failed to come back to replenish his medication. A year passed. During that year Esther and her many supporters in Canada prayed that he would receive Jesus as Savior and Lord. When he returned to the hospital, his lungs were

---

[122] Bill Lyons, "Can You Trust a Smuggler?," *SIMRoots* 36, no. 2 (Fall 2019): 13.
[123] Chris & Helen Cowie, Prayer Letter "Education— Niger—Sahel Academy," September 8, 1986.

in poor condition, and Esther asked him if he had received Jesus yet. His reply was, "No, I'm waiting until I get well."

Knowing that he might not get well, she asked me to visit him and share the gospel again. I had been reading Questions and Answers by Billy Graham about the sin that God does not forgive (John 16:7-11). When I visited Alhaji, I asked him, "Do you know the sin which God will not forgive?" "No," he replied, "you'll have to tell me." I explained that it is rejecting Jesus, whom God sent to pay the price for our sin. A short while later, indicating the seriousness of his intentions, Alhaji softly repeated three times, "I want Jesus. I want Jesus. I want Jesus." Then he prayed to receive Jesus.

The next day when I gave the usual greeting, "How did you sleep?" he replied, "Well. Yesterday…" He paused for several deep breaths, "Yesterday I didn't know where I was with God, but today, I know. I've been forgiven!"

The next morning I asked him how he was, and he said, "I didn't sleep last night. I've been in darkness but now I've come to the light!" Later as I shared truths about heaven with him, Alhaji lifted his hands toward heaven and said, "If God calls me today or tomorrow or the next day, praise the Lord!" When I asked if I could share his story, he simply said, "Tell everyone!"

Alhaji died a few short months later, but his testimony is still a powerful witness to the transformation that occurs when we enter into relationship with Jesus. The Lord entrusted me with his story and for over 30 years I have continued to "Tell everyone!" believing that God will use

Alhaji's story to help others enter the Kingdom of Heaven.[124]

Money on the Go

In the past, missionaries normally drew their salaries at the finance office in their country of service. The office usually had cash on hand that it had withdrawn from the bank for individual and project needs. Andy Paterson relates how that system broke down when he was assistant treasurer in the Francophone Office. The office in Parakou, Benin was having trouble getting cash from the bank. Andy filled a suitcase with cfa francs and drove from Niamey to the bridge spanning the Niger River, the border between Niger and Benin. He stopped halfway across the bridge, where SIMer Paul Vannatto from Parakou met him and made the handoff. A common expression says that 'truth is stranger than fiction.' This story could have come right out of a novel.[125]

---

[124] Bev Botheras, *Tell Everyone: A Story of One Man's Journey Faith*, March 12, 2023.
[125] Barbie Paterson, "Stories from the Patersons," July 6, 2023.

THE 1990s

The decade was a time of growing hope, optimism, and economic expansion. The end of the Cold War signaled the easing of the nuclear threat and led to the breakup of the Soviet Union, with less competition between the superpowers. The two Germanys were reunited, but the country of Yugoslavia split into bitter warring factions, especially in Bosnia. A peace accord was signed between Israel and the Palestinians in 1993, and another peace plan was approved by a vote and implemented in Northern Ireland in 1998. In Asia, the Taliban gained control of Afghanistan (1996), and Hong Kong returned to Chinese rule (1997). Meanwhile, the first world wide web server was launched in 1990, leading to a revolution in global communications, which was a boon for missionaries who often felt isolated from family and supporters.

For Africa the big news in the 1990s was the end of the apartheid regime in South Africa and the election of Nelson Mandela as president (1994). Mobuto Sese Seko, long-time ruler of Zaire, was deposed in 1997, and the country's name reverted to the Democratic Republic of the Congo. Unfortunately, there were several wars on the continent, notably the genocide of nearly 800,000 Tutsis in Rwanda in 1994 and a brutal civil war in Liberia during most of the decade. In West Africa, a significant event was the 50% devaluation of the cfa franc in January 1994, which resulted in high inflation for a short time but also greater productivity in the cfa zone.

The 1990s in Niger were a time of upheaval and change. The country struggled to implement a democratic transition from the previous military regime. Mahamane Ousmane was elected fourth president of Niger in 1993 but was overthrown in a coup on 27 January 1996 after a deadlock between the president and the parliament (Assemblée Nationale). General Ibrahim Baré Maïnassara took over, but he was assassinated by soldiers as he boarded his helicopter at the airport on 19 April 1999. Elections late in the year put Mamadou Tanja in the presidency before the end of the year.

In the early 1990s SIM work in Niger expanded to two locations at opposite ends of the country: Téra (1992) and N'guigmi (1994). Later in the decade, SIM started work in Dakoro, where Tim and Sue Eckert worked with the Fulani (1995), and Makalondi, where Gary and Joy Freeman started work among the Gourmantché (1999). It was also a time of difficulty and heartache as the EERN divided into three independent groups and relationships between church and mission were severely strained (1990).[126] Eventually, five church bodies formed, known by their acronyms EERN, UEEPN, UEES (Salama), EEI, and ACEN. The first three are more oriented toward the Hausa, the latter toward the Gourmantché, and the EEI is more multi-ethnic, with university students from many Francophone countries in the mother church. During the decade there were strikes, death threats, financial difficulties, and critical illnesses of staff at Galmi Hospital, leading to serious discussions about closing SIM's flagship medical facility in the country. A legacy gift of US$100,000 left by a former patient of Dr. Harold Adolph in the US helped turn the sit-

---

[126] Mahamane, "History and Challenges of the Evangelical Church in Niger, 1923–2013," 244.

uation around.[127] There was also a leadership crisis within SIM Niger, and the mission went without a director for over a year after the departure of Nelson Frève in 1996. In addition to all this, there was an explosion of new churches, missions, and development agencies in the country. Up to the 1990s, only a few missions and churches were officially recognized by the government: those related to SIM, EBM, and the Baptist International Mission. From here on, there would be many new organizations and institutions, thus necessitating the need for a forum in which the different groups could speak with one voice.

Literacy Strengthens the Church

Jonathan and Elaine Burt transferred from Nigeria in 1987 and spent many years in Niger until their retirement in 2021. Most of the time, they lived in one of three towns: Guéshémé, Dogondoutchi, or Dioundiou. While their experience and background were in agricultural development, they discovered a real hunger to learn to read due to the efforts of previous SIM missionaries and the government's push to promote literacy in the area. Thus, they embarked on a sustained program of literacy which lasted the duration of their thirty plus years in the country.

Early on, they realized that many of the literacy materials they inherited from Nigeria were not well designed. The first lesson had five consonants and only one vowel. So, the Burts took some literacy training with SIL and learned to use computer software to develop their own materials. Out of this training, Elaine developed the Bible-based Zuma literacy primer. Zuma means 'honey' in

---

[127] Adolph, *Today's Decisions, Tomorrow's Destiny*, 204–7.

Hausa. These materials were much more user-friendly, and the Burts used them the rest of their time in the country.

In each location where they lived, they supervised and led literacy programs, both in the towns and in rural locations. After 2005, first in Dogondoutchi and later in Dioundiou, they used literacy to help many Christians learn to read, and they supported Christians in small villages who used literacy to share the gospel. They would buy building plots and fields for trained pastors who could then make their living from farming. These pastors then served their communities through the gift of teaching reading. This in turn contributed to the growth and strengthening of many new churches in the Dosso region.[128]

Of Flat Tires and the Sovereignty of God

On 21 September 1992, three months after their move to Téra, the DeValves were on their way home after a week of meetings and shopping in Niamey. They crossed the Niger River on a ferry 60 km north of Niamey then caught the unpaved, rutted road for the remaining 120 km. They hoped to be home before dark, but because of their late start and the condition of the road after the rainy season, the sun was already setting as they approached Téra. Suddenly, the left rear tire went flat. It took a while to change the tire, and they arrived home in the dark.

Téra had no electricity at the time, and it was a hot, humid night. Soon after they had gone to bed, Nancy commented that she felt hot, but thinking it might be the heat, they went to sleep. In the morning, Nancy's temperature was over 101°F. She was light-headed, had a terrific head-

---

[128] Jonathan Burt, "SIM Literacy Work in Dosso Region" (UK, 2023); Betsy Edwards, "Miracle at Mouzoumouzou" (Niger, 1993), SIM Int'l.

ache, and was losing consciousness. John administered a chloroquine treatment the doctor had given them for emergencies. No good. A cool shower did no good, either. Nancy's temperature spiked to 104.2°F! Desperate, John went to the post office where there was a telephone. At that time the only ways to communicate with the outside world were snail mail or an old switchboard telephone that had two lines going out.

John called the SIM Office and caught Pete Johnsen, the doctor, on his way out. Pete told John to bring Nancy to Niamey as fast as possible. John rushed home, found Nancy semi-conscious, threw the still packed suitcases back in the truck, got the kids buckled in, carried Nancy to the car, and took off. As he headed out the gate, he thought, 'Wait, the flat tire!' It had to be fixed before going down that bumpy, washboard, road crisscrossed with gullies from the rains. It took fifteen long minutes to get it fixed. Once on the road, the DeValves could not go fast because of the road conditions. It was nearly three hours of tough going before they approached the Niger River ferry.

In the meantime, SIM colleagues came up with a plan. Jim Knowlton suggested that he, Pete Johnsen, and Pauline Clarke, a nurse, take the office van and head toward Téra to meet the DeValves halfway. They called the Téra post office and had a message sent, but the DeValves had already left and never got it.

As they approached the ferry, John realized he was going to arrive shortly after its departure to the other side. They would have to wait almost an hour for it to return. John did not feel they could wait that long, so he was planning to take a dirt track that paralleled the river into Niamey on the right bank. This road was in poor shape, but it was only 60 km, and John felt they had no choice.

About five minutes from the turnoff to this 'back road,' John saw a white van approaching. He recognized it as the office van. He stopped his vehicle, and Pete jumped in with John. Together the two cars proceeded the rest of the way to Niamey, using the ferry which had waited for them to return with the medical emergency.

In all the excitement, John had not realized that if the flat tire had not delayed them 15 minutes, they would have missed the rescue party that was coming to meet them![129] It turned out that Nancy had cerebral malaria and nearly died, but she perked up as soon as she got to the hospital and was administered intravenous quinine.

African Tea Nights

Kuong Sii and Emily Wong were the first SIM missionaries from Malaysia. They worked in Gouré in the 1990s. Shortly after their arrival, they started what became known as 'African Tea Nights'. These events were held on Saturdays and involved Bible study and discussion. Numbers varied from 10 to 15 every Saturday, and discussions were in French. A number of people came to follow Christ through this event.[130]

A Flight to Remember

It was a dry, dusty day, the 2nd of February 1997. At 20:00, Jim Rendel was at home when he received a call from the Niamey control tower saying there was a message from Ken Singleton, area director of World Vision Niger,

---
[129] Pete and Jackie Johnsen, "Prayer Letter," October 1992, SIM Int'l; John R DeValve, "The Amazing Journey" Journal 11 (September 22, 1992).
[130] Bert Haaga, "Operation Outcry" (SIM Niger, September 1994).

who had traveled to Ménaka, Mali with his family for the weekend. Jim went out to the control tower to call Ken but the reception there was poor. Jim told Ken to switch to the mission frequency, and the message would come through on the radio of the SIMAIR plane. What Jim then heard was that the Singelton's three-year-old son, Peter, had fallen in a thirty-foot well and was unconscious. He needed an emergency evacuation to Niamey. SIMAIR does not normally fly at night, and the Ménaka airstrip had no landing lights, but Jim instructed Ken how to light the runway using car headlights. Jim took off around 22:00. The harmattan was not too bad, there was no moon, and there was a new GPS system in the plane, so Jim was able to go directly to Ménaka, and he could see the car lights as he approached the airstrip. Peter had regained consciousness and knew Jim from previous encounters, so Jim said to him, 'Hi Peter ... How would you like to go on an airplane ride with Uncle Jim?' They took off around midnight and were back in Niamey a little over an hour later with the whole family. Peter was rushed to the French clinic, where he was treated and then evacuated the next day to the UK for further tests and treatment. Fortunately, he survived.[131]

Her Name Was Maimouna

The following story from Nancy DeValve highlights the incredible hospitality and welcome that many SIM missionaries have received from Nigeriens:

> Everything was new and confusing. We had just moved to Téra where we were the only English speakers, the only Americans, and almost the only

---

[131] Rich Schaffer, *Just One SIMAir Story* (Bloomington, IN: iUniverse, 2012), 344–45.

white people. Our Songhai language skills were limited, and we knew only a little about Songhai culture. I had no idea how to act in specific social situations.

One day we were out exploring the town. "Fofo! Mate ni keni?" ("Hello! How are you?") we would call out as we waved to those in the compounds we passed. We enjoyed our walk, but I was feeling overwhelmed by the newness of it all, wondering how I would ever learn to feel at home. Nearing our house, we saw a woman pounding grain in her compound. She had a baby tied to her back, and a little boy was chasing chickens. They were the ages of our children. She invited us into her compound to chat and offered to take me places and show me around.

Her name was Maimouna, and she became a dear friend. True to her word, she started taking me everywhere. I found a warm welcome wherever I went because I was with her. In my journal only three days after arriving in Téra I wrote, "Yesterday I went to the market with Maimouna … We walked, greeting everyone as we went. She showed me around the market, then we bought some things. She told me the words for many things, and I wrote them down."

Maimouna would often come early in the morning and tell me that there was a naming ceremony we needed to go to. When we arrived, she would show me how to greet the men under a canopy in the street. Then we would greet the women preparing food and snacks for the day. Finally, we would go into the inner room where the new mom was sequestered with her baby. Maimouna taught me what to do, how to greet, what to give.

As I watched the events of the day, I would ask her questions and she willingly answered.

It was not unusual for her to come with sadness written on her usually cheerful face. "Our neighbor died," she would say. "We need to go greet the family." Again, she would show me who to greet first, where to sit, and the right kinds of questions to ask. I learned how stoic the Songhai are and how they grieve by sitting together for days recounting stories of their loved one.

Maimouna taught me that in Songhai culture you don't talk about how cute a baby is. Instead, you tease and say that the baby is ugly. So, when her co-wife had a baby, I said he was ugly. She laughed and said, "You don't say that to a baby in your family." That is how I understood that we were now family! There wasn't much we didn't know about each other. We took care of each other's children. We borrowed things from each other. We helped each other in times of need. Sometimes we misunderstood each other, but I don't think we ever got into a big disagreement.

It took a long time for me to feel at home in Téra, to speak Songhai, and to feel comfortable in the culture. But I don't know how I would ever have learned anything if it hadn't been for Maimouna.

The China Connection

The workload has always been heavy at Galmi Hospital, and there have almost never been enough doctors, surgeons, and support personnel to take care of all the needs. During the 1990s, the shortage of surgeons was acute, and Dr. Harold Adolph, a surgeon who also served with SIM in Ethiopia and Liberia, was stationed at Galmi for nine years. Exhausted and feeling the need for help, Harold began to think how he could find another surgeon to help carry the load. He thought about a friend from high school in Shanghai, when he was a missionary kid in China. Dr. Paul Xia had been a medical student of his father's and was about to retire from his post as surgeon in a big city hospital. Harold invited him to serve at Galmi, and God overcame some huge obstacles to make his arrival possible. Dr. Paul and his wife Betty served for four years at Galmi, and Harold Adolph describes those years as 'my heaven'. After their time in Galmi, Dr. Paul and Betty retired in the United States.[132]

More Doctors and Surgeons for Galmi Hospital

The need for doctors and surgeons at Galmi continued, and God provided in amazing ways. A doctor from Nigeria sent a family practice resident, who needed surgical training for his study, to Galmi to help bear the load. His name was Joshua Bogunjoko. After he completed his training, he and his wife, Joanna, also a doctor, served in Galmi for several years, including a stint as hospital director from 2002 to 2006. After the Bogunjokos left Galmi, they served in SIM International in leadership roles, notably as Deputy International Director for Europe and West Africa and then as SIM International Director (2013-2024).[133]

Another provision of God for Galmi was a Swiss doctor that Harold Adolph met at a medical missionary con-

---

[132] Harold Paul Adolph, *What If There Were Windows In Heaven* (Meadville, PA: Christian Faith Publishing, Inc., 2017), 101–4; Harold Paul Adolph, *Surgeon On Call 24-7* (La Vergne: Christian Faith Publishing, Inc., 2018), 141–43.
[133] Adolph, *What If There Were Windows In Heaven*, 104.

ference in Kenya. She was a native French speaker from Switzerland who had worked for the Leprosy Mission in Bangladesh and was between assignments. Galmi needed a French speaker who could start a nurses training school. The Leprosy Mission wanted to have a doctor in Niger! It was a divine appointment. While in Niger, this Swiss doctor made contact with the Hospital Christian Fellowship in Niamey. She invited the Christian medical students there to Galmi for a 'weekend retreat and mission challenge.' Seven students attended, and two of the seven were challenged to pursue missions. One of those was Dr. Yakoubou Sanoussi, who trained to be a surgeon in Galmi, Senegal, and France. Dr. Sanoussi went on to lead the surgical

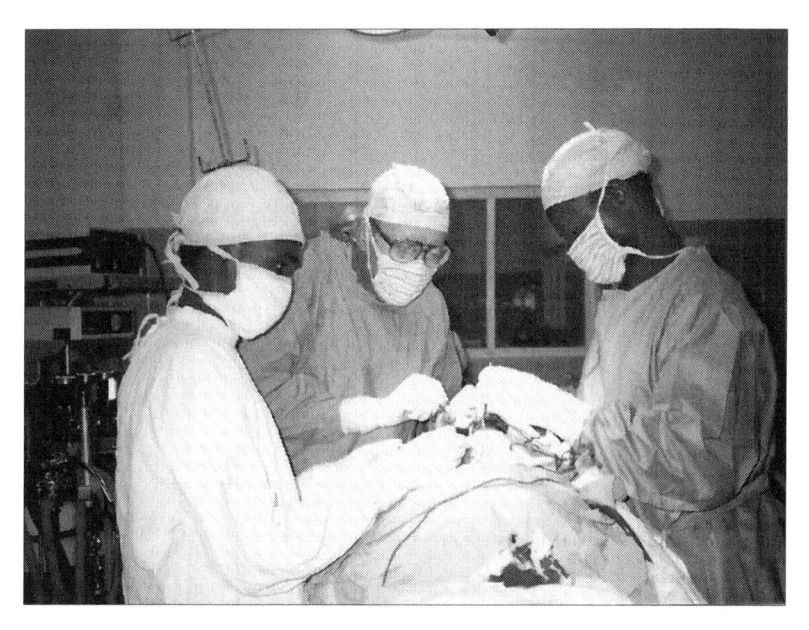

Dr. SANOUSSI Yakoubou (r) assists Dr. Harold ADOLPH in surgery during his first year of surgical training in the PACCS (Pan African College of Christian Surgeons) program at Galmi Hospital. Photo from Today's Decisions, Tomorrow's Destiny, *p. 175.*

training program at Galmi and became the Galmi Hospital director in 2022.[134]

The Formation of AMEEN

One of the most important events of the 1990s was the founding of the Alliance of Evangelical Missions and Churches of Niger (Alliance des Missions et Églises Évangéliques au Niger), known by its French acronym AMEEN. This organization was the result of the birth and growth of new churches and associations in the 1990s. The initial signing of the bylaws and constitution of AMEEN took place on 11 April 1998. There were 17 founding member organizations, and SIM and its five partner churches were original signatories of this association. AMEEN serves as the voice of Niger's evangelical churches before the government and public and is a place for discussion and cooperation on matters that concern Protestant Christians in the country. It serves as a visible expression of the unity of the body of Christ in Niger. Mr. MOUSSA Alassane, a member of the Église Évangélique Internationale (EEI) association—a partner church of SIM—was the first president. He served until his death in 2006.[135]

Accidents Happen

Bert and Elaine Haaga were traveling back to Maïné-Soroa after the annual SIM Niger Conference in Galmi on 3 November 1999. They were approaching Zinder when a rear tire blew out as they were passing some boys walking by the side of the road. The vehicle they were driving was

---
[134] Adolph, *Today's Decisions, Tomorrow's Destiny*, 210–11.
[135] Gordon Evans, "AMEEN Signing," April 10, 1998, SIM Int'l.

a Toyota Hi-Lux, a sturdy, easy to maintain, pickup truck built for rugged terrain in majority world countries. The problem with these vehicles, however, is that they have a high center of gravity and are easy to roll if they are going fast when they encounter rough roads or start to fishtail. Sure enough, because there was no guardrail and there was a 6-foot drop on either side, Bert lost control of the car as it swayed back and forth, and the car rolled onto the passenger side and then onto its top, finally settling on the driver's side. Everyone was able to climb out the broken windshield, and thankfully no one was seriously injured. Nothing had been damaged in the back of the truck, either, not even a laptop and 10 dozen eggs packed in an ice chest! It was protected by a solid wire cage welded to the open back. Passengers from a passing bush taxi helped roll the vehicle onto its wheels, and it was still drivable, a characteristic advantage of these trucks after accidents and mishaps. The family was able to travel on to Zinder, 25 miles further along, where Elaine and the boys caught a bush taxi on to Maïné while Bert stayed on in Zinder for a few days to get the vehicle fixed. Thank the Lord for his mercy and protection in many miles of travel where emergency medical care is often limited.[136]

---

[136] Bert Haaga, "Prayer Letter," November 1999.

THE 2000s

The specter of terrorism became more pronounced and immediate on 11 September 2001 with the attacks on the World Trade Center and the Pentagon in which commercial jetliners were used as weapons. Thousands died, and the world was changed forever. Travel, especially by air, became much more difficult and uncomfortable, and this had a profound effect on missionaries and their preferred mode of travel. What followed during the decade were two wars in Iraq and Afghanistan that did not root out terrorism but succeeded in creating more instability and intensifying dislike for the West. Other terrorist attacks followed in Bali (October 2002), Madrid (March 2004), Russia (September 2004), London (July 2005), Mumbai (July 2006), and other places.

Two big world events of the 2000s were the Indian Ocean earthquake and tsunami in January 2004 that claimed over 225,000 lives and the financial meltdown of 2008 fueled by lax lending and cheap credit that caused a housing bubble. A severe economic crisis followed the latter event, and many people lost jobs, homes, and savings. Some bright spots around the world were the independence of East Timor (May 2002) and the election of the first black president in the United States (Barack Obama) in 2008.

For Africa, it was a calmer decade, although there were plenty of conflicts. The Liberian civil war finally came to an end (August 2003), and Ethiopia and Eritrea signed a peace treaty (December 2000), but conflict continued in Darfur, Sudan and the DRC.

In Niger, a civilian government under his Excellency Mamadou Tanja spanned the entre decade. He was overthrown in a coup on 18 February 2010 when he tried to change the constitution to extend his mandate beyond the two-term limit. Aside from some mutinies in the army, this period seemed peaceful and calm, belying the events in the rest of the world.

New ministries for SIM Niger in the decade included a Bible College, initially called ESTEN (École Supérieure de Théologie Évangélique de Niamey) but later changed to ESPriT (École Supérieure Privée de Théologie), which started in 2003. The college trains pastors and leaders for Benin, Burkina Faso, Niger, and other countries and grants bachelor's degrees in theology. Another new initiative was the Christian Education project started by Ben Hegeman, Brigitte Pini, and Gordon and Judy Evans. The next chapter will tell some of the story of this initiative. During the decade, Bruce & Robin Walton and family moved to Tchin-Tabaraden north of Tahoua to work among the Touareg (2001). And a big change occurred when the annual spiritual life conference was moved from Galmi, where it had been held for decades, to Niamey in January 2002 under the direction of Linda Watt. In late 2004, SIM celebrated 80 years in the country. Many retired missionaries came to celebrate the occasion. In 2005, Sahel Academy received a large influx of staff and students from Côte d'Ivoire when International Christian Academy (ICA) closed because of civil war. Brian Bliss, one of the staff at ICA, eventually became the Sahel Academy director and served in that capacity until 2014.

Maradi Riots

November 9th, 2000 dawned much like any other day in Maradi. The day before, a conservative Muslim group had held a peaceful demonstration in Niamey against an international fashion show. The same group decided to hold a second march in Maradi on November 9th. Unlike the protest the previous day, however, this demonstration was anything but peaceful. As one protestor remarked, 'We don't want to hurt anyone. We just want to do as much damage as possible.'

And damage they did. The marchers targeted churches, bars, lottery kiosks, and houses of ill repute, leaving many people—especially women—homeless. Normally the safest thing to do during a march like this would have been to shelter at home. This was anything but a normal protest, however. After attacking the next-door Vie Abondante (Abundant Life) Church and burning it, the mob turned on the SIM mission compound. It was the first time in SIM Niger's 75-odd year history that anything like this had happened. The rioters were bent on destroying everything in sight and tried to break into buildings. When they started to set fire to the houses, Susan, Kara, and Ellen Strong (Andrew was away) escaped out the back fence and found refuge elsewhere. Another missionary, Beng Kuan Tan, was in the office when the mob attacked and struggled to exit the building before some Nigerien workers helped her. Thankfully, the workers managed to limit the damage and put out fires quickly. Only three vehicles were damaged or burned.

There were some positive results of the riots. First, churches became more recognized by the authorities and people in Maradi. Second, a wall around the compound was built in 2005-2006, replacing the insecure fence. Tim Eckert and Andrew Strong supervised the building of this wall. The wall gave a more secure, home-like feeling to the compound. By that point, many homes and businesses in the area already had walls around them. Third, many local people came to express their sadness and condolences after the senseless destruction. Fourth, the authorities took swift action in arresting the riot leaders. This was a huge precedent because after the terrorist attacks in New York and Washington in September 2001, the government took similar action to arrest leaders of conservative groups making threats against churches, Christians, and outside interests.[137]

Show and Tell Nigerien Style

Wanda and Randy Potratz spent several years in Niger. They worked in IT and at Sahel Academy as well as in literacy work. The Potratzes had good working relationships with the African staff who worked to clean and maintain the Sahel campus. In 2001, Wanda was teaching first grade at Sahel. She had eight students from five countries: Canada, France, Nigeria, Norway, and the US. There was a knock at the screen door, and there stood one of the cleaners, Songli, with a dead monitor lizard in his arms. The lesson Wanda was teaching was cut short so that the first graders could have an impromptu science lesson. Later, the dead lizard became lunch for some of the hungry workers on campus.[138]

---

[137] Tim & Sue Eckert, "Eckert Extra," Prayer Letter, December 2000; Susan Strong, "Building Walls" (Australia, June 2, 2023).
[138] Randy Potratz, "Lizard for Lunch," July 31, 2023.

The Maza Tsaye Center of Ministries

Burned out after a term of leading the SIM Niger field, Gordon and Judy Evans wondered if they could return to Niger for another term when they left for home assignment in 2002. God renewed their vision and strength, and they returned the following year for another term as director, but this time, they devoted Wednesdays to prayer and fasting. In the morning, they set aside time to pray at home, and in the afternoon, they met with Nigerien pastors and their wives to pray. Out of these prayer meetings, they heard two heart cries. The first was the need for marriage training for couples and the second was the need for a good education for their children. It was out of these prayer meetings that two ministries at Maza Tsaye near Maradi were born. The story of the educational ministries will be related in the next chapter. Here, we will tell the story of the Maza Tsaye Center of Ministries.

In 2004, during Gordon's second term as director, Donald and Lorraine Gingras of the Canadian Revival Fellowship went to Niger from Canada to conduct a marriage retreat for church leaders and their wives. Twenty couples attended this first retreat. Some of the comments showed the value of this kind of training.

> *This retreat has given us the tools to repair our broken relationship and renew our love for one another.*

> *We are committing to the path of humility and mutual forgiveness in order to glorify the Lord.*

Near the end of Gordon's second term as director, he and Judy began to look for a place in the middle of the country that could serve as a retreat center and training location. They stumbled upon the old SIM farm school—later a preparatory Bible School—in Maza Tsaye in July 2005. They realized the potential of this old site as a centre for the renewal, encouragement, and equipping of the Nigerien church. After Gordon stepped down as director, they moved to Maza Tsaye in October 2007, and they held a consecration ceremony in November to restore the former farm school into a retreat center. They found encouragement and inspiration in Isaiah 58:12, which became the theme verse of the center. It says in part, 'Those from among you shall build the old waste places; You shall raise up the foundations of many generations.'

Original building at Maza Tsaye, 2005

Since then, most of the buildings have been renovated and renewed, and a large pavilion was erected on the

Maza Tsaye Center in 2023

property. A wall was constructed around most of the property, and kitchen and bathroom facilities were upgraded. The center has touched hundreds of lives through kids' clubs, marriage retreats, conferences, sporting events, training events for youth, and a feeding program for babies. Churches and missionaries have used the center for many different programs and events, including weddings.[139]

A Hot Flight

Humidity, heat, and weight can all be detrimental to the lift of an airplane when it takes off. On one particular flight piloted by Jim Rendel from Galmi to Niamey in 2007, the six-seater Piper was loaded with four people, including two returning doctors, and quite a bit of luggage. Jim had decided to leave some luggage behind because of the weight. Randy Potratz, who was one of the passengers, was returning to Niamey after a trip servicing the Galmi Hospital computers. He takes up the story.

> I was fortunate to be able to sit in the right-hand seat and had a headset so I could communicate with Jim easily. During the taxi out he made a comment about someone building a house at the end of the runway fairly recently and he was not particularly happy about that. We made our way towards the far end of the runway … [Jim] intently watched the windsock on that end. It was a pretty lazy windsock. We watched it for what seemed like a couple of minutes … praying for some wind.
>
> [There was] a slight breeze from a direction that was beneficial to us. Then [the windsock] be-

---
[139] Judy Evans, "Maza Tsaye Centre of Ministries—The Story of God's Amazing Goodness & Faithfulness," August 9, 2023.

came more active. Jim [set] the throttle to full and [turned] the plane, heading towards the east, down the runway. There was tension as some of us had an idea we were probably close to limits with the heat, the humidity, the lack of a decent wind, and the load.

There is a gap in the trees at the edge of the Galmi runway about the halfway point where the plane comes to a stop and is loaded. Usually when you pass that spot on takeoff, you can feel the plane just starting to grip the air and [become] an airplane. I didn't feel it this time.

About three-quarters [of the way down the runway], I started noticing the lift. I looked over at Jim. "We're going to use every foot of this runway," he noted matter-of-factly. He might have said "inch." This was strangely reassuring. At least I did not hear anything about needing more runway.

We cleared the east wall of the runway with some altitude to spare. The Lord knows if it was feet or inches. And the guy who had built the house at the end of the runway? I will always have the picture in my mind of him looking up, genuinely startled, and maybe a bit scared, from the backside of his house. For his part, Jim just looked over at me as we were climbing out and gave a quick half smile.[140]

Another SIMAIR Story

Of all the adventures that SIMAIR pilots have had, one of the most singular was searching for a missing person in the Sahara. It was the end of March 2006, the time when

---

[140] Randy Potratz, "Jim Rendel and the Very Hot Day," July 31, 2023.

a total solar eclipse passed over Niger. Many tourists came to Niger to see the eclipse, and some wanted to see it from the desert. They rented all the four-wheel drive vehicles in Agadez—all 400 of them!—and drove out into the Sahara. A man whom we'll call Ali, a mechanic who works in Agadez and doesn't normally drive into the desert, was hired to carry water and food to the tourists and repair any cars which had broken down. On the way into the desert, he was in a caravan, but on the way back to Agadez, he traveled with some trucks. The wind was blowing fiercely, and Ali got separated from the trucks and took a wrong turn into the desert. The trucks tried to find him without success. Likewise, search teams and the military searched but did not find him.

It was time for SIMAIR to have a go at locating Ali. The tourism company called and asked if SIMAIR could help. Ian Rideout, one of the pilots, fueled the plane and took off for Agadez, a three-hour flight from Niamey. Along with Ian was an experienced guide/pilot/hotelier named Julia Akli. The weather cleared over the search area even though it was dusty to the south. After Agadez, Ian then piloted the plane to the east into the Ténéré Desert. It took four and a half hours of flying back and forth across the desert before they located the truck and Ali, who was waving at them and very much alive. They radioed his coordinates to waiting vehicles on the ground, and it wasn't long until those vehicles located and rescued him. It was amazing that they found him because he was located between big rocks on one side and sand dunes on the other. It would have been almost impossible for vehicles on the ground to find him.[141]

---

[141] Ian Rideout, "Report on Air Rescue," May 2023.

An Integrated Model of Member Care

On Thursday, 8th January 2009, missionaries were returning to their places of ministry after the annual SIM Niger Spiritual Life Conference. One car was traveling to Galmi with Nigerian doctor Musa dan Kyau, Japanese nurse Yoko Yoshioko, Swiss teacher Laurence Moret, and Singaporean doctor and mission leader Andrew Ng. Musa dan Kyau was at the wheel. Near Dogondoutchi, a teenage boy darted out from behind a parked bus into the car's path. Musa swerved but couldn't avoid striking the boy, hit an embankment on the far side of the road, rolled three times, and landed upright facing Niamey. Unfortunately, the boy died.

Andrew and Laurence sustained only minor injuries. Musa was briefly knocked unconscious. When he came to, he and Andrew crawled out the broken front windows beside their seats. Yoko's injuries were more serious, with a contusion and sustained head injuries. She was in the back seat collapsing onto Laurence's lap, and it took some strong local men to open the car doors to free them.

A passing car took Yoko and Musa to the hospital in Dogondoutchi. Meanwhile, another car with Sonya Durrenmatt and Ruth Perkins stopped and picked up the luggage from the wrecked car. A third car with Dr. Matt Megill and family and Linda Hardy also stopped to give assistance. Yoko was sent to Niamey by ambulance with Matt and Ruth attending her. She was taken to the Clinique Alissa, where she was cared for around the clock by SIM medical personnel and by Dr. Samaila Sanoussi, a Christian neurosurgeon who operated on her to remove blood clots and stanch bleeding on the brain. Later, a doctor in the UK evaluated Yoko after her recovery from surgery.

Back in Niamey, Belinda Ng, informed that her husband Andrew was in the accident, was able to contact him and learn he was okay. At the same time, an MK education conference was beginning in Niamey, with Belinda presenting. The people attending the conference, upon hearing the news, immediately stopped and prayed for all those in the accident. Mobile Member Care Team Psychologist Karen Carr was at the conference. She debriefed Belinda and then flew to Galmi to debrief those involved. Belinda was able to contact families, prayer partners, and SIM leaders in Japan and Singapore to inform them what had happened. It is astounding to realize how people from so many different nationalities, professions, and backgrounds cooperated in a coordinated effort to care for and assist the victims of this accident.[142] This shows the multi-ethnic, international character of SIM.

---

[142] Belinda Ng, "An Integrated Model of Member Care – Niger," July 11, 2023.

THE 2010s

The 2010s were marked by conflict and natural disaster. Syria descended into civil war starting in 2011. So did South Sudan in 2013, after it gained independence from Sudan in 2011. When the US pulled out of Iraq in 2011, it left a power vacuum, and the ISIS (ISIL) extremist group invaded the northern part of the country and set up a violent 'caliphate' in 2014, which lasted for three years. There were major earthquakes in Haiti in 2010, Japan in 2011, and Nepal in 2015. Another major event of the decade was Brexit, the departure of the UK from the European Union (EU). The citizens of the UK voted narrowly to leave the EU on 23 June 2016, and after protracted negotiations, completed the separation on 31 December 2020.

Terrorism continued in the 2010s and seemed to target Africa especially. Countries hit hard by violence included Kenya—where Al Shabab attacked a Nairobi shopping mall in 2013 and killed more than 70, Nigeria—where Boko Haram kidnapped over 200 schoolgirls in 2014, and the Sahel—where increased Islamic militancy destabilized the region and led to the division of Mali into two separate entities. Other places that experienced terrorism were Pakistan—with the killing of around 150 by the Taliban at a school in 2014, and Paris—with the Charlie Hebdo murders of Jan 2015 and the attacks on a stadium and a theater in November of the same year that killed over 130. Sri Lanka also experienced an Easter Sunday attack on churches that killed over 250 in 2019. Home-grown terrorists killed 77 in Norway (2011), 58 in Las Vegas (2017), and over 50 in New Zealand (2019).

Instability, poverty, and corruption led to a huge migrant/refugee crisis from 2014 to 2019. Millions of people tried to escape war, hunger, and persecution in places like Syria, Somalia, and West Africa. Many spent large sums of money and encountered terrible deprivations and dangers as they attempted to traverse the Sahara or large bodies of water like the Mediterranean Sea to reach Europe and the expectation of a better life. The flood of refugees overwhelmed European countries and led to a backlash and prejudice against the new arrivals.

In Africa, the decade was marked by two major events. The first was the Arab Spring, which started in North Africa in 2010 and succeeded in deposing dictators in Tunisia, Algeria, Libya, and Egypt as well as other countries in the Arab World. The Arab Spring had limited effect, however, as it did not necessarily implement better governance. It also led to civil war and instability in Libya, which in turn contributed to gun and drug running and people smuggling and strengthened the growing extremist movements in the Sahara. The second event was the Ebola epidemic in West Africa in 2014-2015. Over 11,000 people died in the worst outbreak of the disease in history, particularly in the countries of Liberia, Sierra Leone, and Guinea. One other event of the decade in Africa was the overthrow of Omar al-Bashir, longtime dictator of Sudan, in 2019.

For Niger, this decade was mostly peaceful and free of major political upheaval. After the coup in February 2010 and subsequent elections, one single government was in power for the rest of the decade, and his Excellency President Mahamadou Issoufou was able to govern without much interference from the military or other parties.

There was increasing Islamic militant activity in the north, and in 2016, a man from another mission—Jeff Woodke—became the first missionary kidnapped in Niger. There were two big events that occurred in the 2010s. One was the flood of 2012, when the Niger River topped the dikes on the right bank in Niamey and inundated and destroyed many homes and businesses. Sahel Academy and the Centre Biblique campuses both had two to six feet of water in them, and a costly process of rehabilitation ensued which lasted a year. The other major event was the reaction to the Charlie Hebdo terrorist attack in Paris and the support the Niger president gave to protest terrorism. In Niger this resulted in attacks on perceived French and 'Christian' targets on 16-17 January 2015. Over 80 churches were burned and/or destroyed in the attacks, and the SIM property in Gouré was levelled.

SIM in Niger was increasingly limited by the growing extremist activity during the decade. Missionaries had to withdraw from many places in the east and could no longer travel to places in the west. By the end of the decade, SIM people were confined to the major centers of Niamey, Maradi, and Galmi, with a few outlying areas like Dioundiou and places near Maradi. Main ministries included Sahel Academy, Galmi Hospital, SIMAIR, ESPriT, Danja Fistula and Leprosy Center, Maza Tsaye Center of Ministries, gospel witness in the cities and outlying areas, Bible translation, and the administrative offices in Niamey. One new initiative of the decade was the beginning of the Fulfulde Ministry Training Center in 2010. Tim and Sue Eckert and Phil and Carol Short were instrumental in helping start this Bible training school, and in 2023, it is solely under the direction of Fulfulde speakers.

The Launching of an Association of Christian Schools and Cornerstone Academy

As reported in the last chapter, one of the cries of pastors and evangelists in Niger in the 2000s was the concern for their children's education. This need led to the formation of the general education initiative in SIM Niger in 2004. Over the next several years, this initiative invited Christian educators, notably Jim Vreugdenhil of Canada, to conduct teacher training seminars in Niger. The first of these seminars was held in the summer of 2005. As a result, a new organization, the Cornerstone Association of Christian Schools (Association Cornerstone), was formed in 2006. Meanwhile, Gordon and Judy Evans had moved to Maza Tsaye in 2007 with a vision to rehabilitate the former farm school and start a center for ministries as well as a Christian school. This school, while not an SIM owned institution, came under the umbrella of the Cornerstone Association, and the Evans were instrumental in starting it. In 2012 a portion of the Maza Tsaye property was set aside for the construction of an elementary and secondary school. In the meantime, classes began that same year at the newly minted Cornerstone Academy with a kindergarten class in rented facilities on the property. Subsequent grades were added each year to allow the first class to continue its education at the school. The first three-classroom block was completed in January 2015, and the faculty and students were delighted to move into the new building.

A major crisis erupted at the school in September 2016 when five of the six teachers scheduled to teach the next school year had to step back from their commitments, leaving the school without adequate staff just before the start of the school year. Within three weeks, God had provided four volunteers, none of them teachers, but all with high educational qualifications, some better than those who had been lined up to teach originally. SIM Education Consultant Laurence Moret moved from Niamey to Maradi to help train the new teachers. In November of that year, the Education Ministry in Niamey approved the application for authorization of Cornerstone Academy.

By 2023, Cornerstone Academy had over 250 students in kindergarten through grade 10 (3^e). The elementary students were meeting in their own classrooms, and the secondary students met in the Maza Tsaye Center's seminar rooms while awaiting construction of their own classrooms. The elementary curriculum includes French immersion materials from Canada, easy step readers, the daily five (*5 au quotidien*), and laminated exercise sheets. All the grade 10 students in 2023 passed the government exams to go into high school. This has helped reinforce the reputation of Cornerstone Academy as a quality school. Being a quality Christian school in Niger has given the staff the opportunity to share God's Word and truth through rigorous academics, Christian lives, Bible curriculum, and memorizing Scripture. In June 2023, Cornerstone Academy was formally transferred to the leadership of Association Cornerstone (Niamey), the mother Cornerstone branch, which now has four schools across the country.[143]

---

[143] Judy Evans, "Académie Evangelique Cornerstone Maradi, the Crown Jewel of all the Maza Tsaye Ministries," August 9, 2023.

The Beginning of PAACS at Galmi

The Pan African Academy of Christian Surgeons (PAACS) developed from discussions among missionary surgeons in 1996 at a continuing medical education conference in Kenya. Intense workloads, difficulty in recruitment of long-term medical missionaries, and previous experiences mentoring national doctors both spiritually and professionally stirred a vision of developing a systematic program of spiritual discipleship integrated with an accredited surgical training program in mission hospitals. One of the missionary surgeons who was a part of that discussion was Harold Adolf, a SIM missionary, working at Galmi Hospital. The PAACS program at Galmi started with two residents from Madagascar and one Nigerien (Yakoubou Sanoussi). Unfortunately, in late 1997, Dr. Adolf had to leave the field due to vision loss from macular degeneration. At that point in time, no missionary surgeon could be found to take over the program, so it was forced to close. The residents from Madagascar returned home and used the skills they had learned at Galmi for the remainder of their career. Dr. Sanoussi completed his surgical training in Senegal and then in France. In 2009, Dr. Sanoussi met with Dr. Joe Starke in France as Yakoubou was completing his training and Joe was in language school with plans to serve in Niger. They discussed the possibility of restarting a PAACS general surgery residency at Galmi. Working with SIM Niger, Galmi Hospital administration, and PAACS over the next two years they were able to see the Lord open the doors for the program to be reestablished in 2012. To date the program has graduated 10 surgeons who are serving in mission hospitals in Liberia, Kenya, Burundi, and Niger.[144]

---

[144] Joe Starke, "The Beginnings of PAACS," March 8, 2024.

Sahel Academy Accreditation

In 2007, a school board was created to manage and direct the affairs of Sahel Academy. Over the next few years, the board initiated the process of accreditation for the school. The goal of accreditation was to certify the academic standing of the school so that Sahel students would have a formally accepted education in their home countries. One of the milestones of the 2010s was the completion of this task after years of preparation, self-study, and the updating of the curriculum guide. A team visited the school in February 2012 to assess its readiness for accreditation. Reporting back favorably, the team recommended that Sahel Academy be accredited by both the Middle States Association and the Association of Christian Schools International (ACSI). This milestone was achieved in October of that same year under the leadership of director Brian Bliss assisted by a host of board members, educators, parents, staff, and students.[145]

Church Burnings of 2015

The church burnings of January 2015 were one of the defining moments of the 2010s for Christians in Niger. Not only the churches, but also missionaries were hit hard by this crisis. In Gouré, where the church and the SIM mission compound were destroyed, no missionaries were present on the compound when the mobs attacked, but they and the Christians in town lost all their possessions. It was a hard blow even for those who once lived in the town but had left in the years just prior to the attacks. For Andrew

---

[145] Brian & Cathy Bliss, "News Updates," *SIMRoots*, 2010; Mikki Schmidt, "Accreditation of Sahel Academy," October 30, 2023.

and Susan Strong, it brought up old trauma. Almost fifteen years earlier, Susan and the girls had witnessed the riots in Maradi. Later, they lived in Gouré for a number of years, but they had to leave Niger due to Andrew's health in 2009. On January 16, 2015, the Strongs began receiving frantic calls and texts from friends in Gouré whose property was being destroyed and whose lives were being threatened as rioters went through the town looting and burning. The SIM youth center, homes, and businesses were destroyed in addition to the church and missionary compound. The Strongs felt immense sorrow as they mourned with their African brothers and sisters and grieved again over the loss of their home and ministry in Niger. One hopeful outcome of the riots in Gouré was the meeting called by the sous-préfet (local government leader) to reprimand the rioters and try to bring reconciliation between Christians and Muslims. Other churches were attacked that day in places like Zinder, Tanout, and Maradi.[146]

Meanwhile, in Niamey on the following day, Saturday, 17 January, Nancy DeValve had gone out looking for tires. Her husband. John had traveled to Téra the previous day to do some research and had had a flat tire. The spare was also flat, and he had no way to repair the tires in Téra. John had called Nancy to ask if she could find a tire for him and send it up on a bush taxi. So Nancy went out with a Nigerien taxi man to look for tires. They went to a tire place downtown, and it was closed. This seemed odd for a Saturday morning, but the taxi man said he knew of another place in the Nouveau Marché quartier. As they started driving there, Nancy noticed smoke in the air and saw tanks and other armed vehicles. This was disturbing, and she called

---

[146] Strong, "Building Walls," 2–3.

Mobs burn the benches and equipment from a church in Niamey on 17 January 2015.

the security officer, Jon Banke, who told her to return home immediately. Mobs were out in the streets looting and burning lottery kiosks, police vehicles, the commissariat, hotels, and bars. They attacked, burned, and gutted over 70 churches in Niamey, both Catholic and Protestant. Most of the damage was done in a two-hour period. The president of the country at the time, his Excellency Mahamadou Issoufou, condemned the attacks and is quoted as saying to the Nigerien people, 'What have the Christians of Niger done to deserve this? Where have they wronged you?' Several prominent Christian leaders, including those in the Catholic Church, the EERN, and the AMEEN, publicly forgave the perpetrators of the destruction and violence. No known Christians were killed by the mobs, but many were threatened, and ten Nigeriens lost their lives as a result of the attacks and ensuing conflagrations. While the mobs consisted mainly of young men, many Muslims stood up for Christians, sheltering those threatened with harm and protecting property held by Christians.[147]

Trauma Healing

One of the ministries that came to prominence in the 2010s was the ministry of trauma healing. Spurred on by the epidemic of Ebola in West Africa, by war and civil strife, by poverty and domestic violence, and by natural disaster all over the continent, the ministry took shape in Niger through the engagement and direction of Linda Watt and Gaston Slanwa. These two leaders attended a workshop in Cameroon in 2014, and the training proved timely and effective as they debriefed many pastors following the church burnings in January 2015. They went on to train around fifty pastors in trauma heling later that year, and Linda organized a children's trauma healing event for pastors' kids.[148]

Speech, Speech

The FEU (Foyer Évangélique Universitaire) or Student Ministry Center started as a SIM ministry to university students in Niamey in 1998. It was the brainchild of Scott

---

[147] Miriam Diez Bosch, "Niger: Their Enemies Burn Their Churches ... and They Forgive Them," *Aleteia*, April 11, 2015, https://aleteia.org/2015/04/11/niger-their-enemies-burn-their-churches-and-they-forgive-them/; Josh Heikkila, "Muslims Stand with Christians against Attacks on Churches in Niger," *Presbyterian Church (USA) News*, February 25, 2015, https://www.pcusa.org/news/2015/2/25/muslims-stand-christians-against-attacks-churches-/; "70+ Churches Destroyed as 'Anti-Charlie' Protests Spread in Niger," *World Watch Monitor*, January 20, 2015, https://www.worldwatchmonitor.org/2015/01/70-churches-destroyed-as-anti-charlie-protests-spread-in-niger/.
[148] Milton Watt, "Ministry of Milton and Linda Watt in Niger," July 31, 2023, 2, Email.

and Lucia Eberle and Eliane Martinez. The FEU has only employed a handful of people and has relied mostly on volunteers, both missionaries and Christian students, to run it. One of the missionaries who volunteered at the FEU was Randy Potratz. After several years of teaching IT classes, Randy took on some of the leadership roles, officially becoming the director in 2019. In the late 2010s, the FEU offered evening and weekend courses in such things as office software, cooking, and leadership, but the most popular courses were the multiple levels of English classes. Here is Randy's story of one event held at the FEU in which he had to speak in French, a language that is not his mother tongue.

> One evening we held an appreciation ceremony in which we awarded class certificates and had a meal. I thought it would be culturally appropriate for the director to give a few words of thanks. I felt comfortable with my French in one-on-one settings at that point, and if there was a misunderstanding, I could resolve that during the conversation. If I was speaking in French to a larger group, however, it was much harder to gauge comprehension if I did not express the concepts well. So, I carefully wrote down everything I wanted to say on a few index cards and practiced the short speech a few times.
>
> When the time came to deliver the speech, I was nervous. I prayed. With some trepidation, I began reading from the first card. It was horrible. It was wooden. I stumbled over some of the words. Looking up at the faces, I knew they felt embarrassed for me. "God, what should I do?" I quickly prayed. In frustration I threw the cards in the air and restarted, but this time I used simple words,

speaking directly to the students. As I did, there were cheers and claps! In the end, my second try was well received, and I learned a few lessons. First, a few simple words from the heart are more important to people than a scripted statement. Secondly, most people will give you great grace when you are speaking their language as a second language. In most instances they are very happy you are making the effort. Lastly, you can trust God to help you learn from missteps if you are willing to be flexible.[149]

Physiotherapy at Danja Health Center

Physiotherapy has been an integral part of SIM medical ministries at Galmi, Danja, and elsewhere. The following story comes from Michelle Pieké, who spent five years in Danja between 2012 and 2020.

> Sa'idou was minding his cattle out in the bush when he was attacked by bandits. He was bound up, and by the time he was found three hours later, he had lost circulation to his hands and feet. He went to several other hospitals before going to Danja, but no one could do anything to save his limbs. The first thing we [had to do] for Sa'idou was to amputate both hands and one foot. I fully expected Sa'idou to be in a heavy depression following this dramatic surgery, but he showed remarkable peace, and I knew he was a fighter. As the incisions on his arms started to heal, we started experimenting with arm cuffs with different attachments. On his first try he was able to use a spoon and fed himself again from that day forth.

---

[149] Randy Potratz, "Speech, Speech, Speech at the FEU," July 31, 2023.

For two months we tried to save his second foot, but the wounds were bone deep and the foot was more painful than it was helpful. Though it was a difficult decision, it was agreed that it was better to remove this foot too. [After the surgery], Sa'idou was no longer plagued by pain for the first time in six months. [Instead], he got up and walked! It was so exciting to be bringing hope and healing out of what seemed like a hopeless and helpless situation.[150]

Michelle also used her skills at the fistula center, helping women who had suffered pain and incontinence from difficult deliveries. Here is a brief story of one of those ladies.

[When] Amina came to the fistula clinic, [she] had severe leg pain and a profound limp, so she joined us for exercises under the tree. Thankfully, Amina's pain settled quickly, and she soon underwent successful surgery. Because her pelvic floor muscles were weak, though, she was still incontinent. Nothing could hold Amina back, however! She started going for longer and longer walks, and with all of this exercise, both her pelvic floor muscles and her hip muscles strengthened quickly. When her family came to visit, they saw her first from a distance and didn't recognize her because she was no longer limping. In fact, she even ran after our deaf gardener because he didn't hear her calling![151]

---

[150] Michelle Pieké, "Moving Toward Hope: Physiotherapy at CSL+DFC Danja," July 26, 2023, 2.
[151] Ibid., Pieké, 3.

New Testament Dedications

During the decade, SIM, in conjunction with SIL, completed work on three translations of the New Testament. The first of these was the Tamajaq translation in the Tawallammat dialect. Many people collaborated on this New Testament, both mother tongue translators and missionaries and it was dedicated in January 2016. Another team of mother tongue translators, under the direction of Jean Baumbach, completed the translation of the New Testament in the eastern Fulfulde dialect in September 2016. The third translation was the western dialect of Fulfulde, completed in 2018 and dedicated in February 2019. It was begun by Steve and Ann White of SIL and finished by a team of mother tongue speakers facilitated by Milton Watt. Milton also trained as a translation consultant and helped teams working on over two dozen translation projects around the world. SIM continues to work on translation of the Old Testament in the three languages mentioned as well as the translation of the Bible into other Nigerien languages.

THE 2020s

The world entered the 2020s on a dark note. A new disease rapidly grabbed headlines and marched across the globe. What eventually became known as COVID-19 shut down world travel and caused panic and death on a massive scale. An economic recession accompanied the pandemic and threw global commerce into confusion from which it was still recovering in 2023. Several major wars erupted at the beginning of the decade, leading to more disruption and destruction. The most important of these were the Russia-Ukraine War—which started in February 2022, the war in Sudan between various factions of the armed forces—which begun in April 2023, and the Hamas-Israel War—which started after the terrorist attacks by Hamas in Israel on 7 October 2023. There was more political and social chaos when the US withdrew from Afghanistan in late August 2022. And the longest reigning monarch in UK history, Elizabeth II, died on 08 September 2022. Her life spanned most of the century of SIM's work in Niger.

For Africa, there were coup d'états in several countries in the Francophone community, first in Mali (2020), then Guinea (2021), Burkina Faso (two coups in 2022), and Gabon (2023). Mali and Burkina Faso asked all French troops to leave, and relations with the former colonial power deteriorated. Terrorism, banditry, and rebel activity increased across the Sahel and the Sahara in the decade, throttling the movement of people and goods, and creating a refugee crisis. After experiencing the first democratic transition of power in its history in 2021, Niger's military followed the example of its neighbors and staged a coup d'état in July 2023.

Two other major events have defined the decade so far. The first was an increase in terrorism. The ghastly murder of six French aid workers and their driver and guide while visiting the giraffe preserve outside Niamey in August 2020 engendered more restrictions on aid groups and western people. Specifically, SIM Niger people were faced with travel restrictions and a mandate to travel with armed guards across the country. The second defining event was the flood of 2020, which came in two stages in August and September when two different sections of the dike along the Niger River in Niamey broke, flooding different parts of Haro Banda. Sahel Academy, the EEI Church at Centre Biblique, ESPriT, and various missionaries were forced out of their homes, some of them twice. As a result, Sahel Academy and the EEI decided to relocate their campuses away from the river. For various reasons, ESPriT chose to remain on the Centre Biblique campus but spent a year in exile while the campus was repaired. Floods and the resultant destruction of properties and fields were also reported in other parts of the country.

Missionaries from West Africa

One of the encouraging trends of this decade was the increasing numbers of missionaries coming from neighboring West African countries and from Niger itself. It started in the 1990s with the arrival of people like the Bogunjokos (Galmi) and the Olulotos (Danja) and accelerated in the following decades. Dozens of missionaries from West

African countries have served in Niger since 2000, particularly from Nigeria, where a common language (Hausa) facilitates their adaptation and ministry.

SIM NIGER
AREA DIRECTOR MESSAGES

We asked each SIM Niger area director (AD) from 1991 to 2023 to reflect on their time as director and comment about the role they had during their mandate and their hopes for the future. Here are their remarks:

Reflections on My Time as Director

Nelson Frève (1991-1996)

Greetings to all my SIM Niger family! What a joy it is for me to be able to share what I'm struggling to remember about my tenure as the Niger AD. Thanks to Carolyn, my dear wife of 48 years whose memory is phenomenal, Wendy Brown (the world's greatest secretary), and my dear friend Tony Rinaudo for their contributions.

The Birth of Triplets

No, the triplets weren't born at Galmi; they were born in 1992 in the hallowed halls of SIM International. The SIM Francophone area (Benin, Burkina Faso, and Niger) had grown to the point where it became necessary to split the three countries into separate administrative entities. This separation was necessary to become more effective and efficient in achieving our objectives, including providing better missionary care. As a result, what used to be called Francophone Area Council (FAC) became Niger Area Council (NAC). It took time to adjust to the changes. Policies that once applied to all three countries now needed to be adapted for each country. Some may recall how we tangled over a water cooler policy at NAC! We were also involved in trying to find a peaceful solution for labor disputes at Galmi Hospital, a problem that was engendered in part by the birth of the triplets.

Station Managers to Teams
One of the challenges we had during this period was to ensure that teams were able to meet for encouragement, prayer, and planning. At that time, we were divided into geographical areas overseen by station managers. Although this worked well for encouragement and prayer, our ethnic teams and institutions were not meeting for strategic planning, hence the notion that we divide into teams. As with all changes, this was not easy at first, nor was it perfect. This change afforded opportunities for teams to meet and to strategize, but it meant that regions were no longer meeting together.

Rural Development
1991 – 1996 was a period of growth and expansion for the MIDP (Maradi Integrated Development Project). Key players in the MIDP were Ruth Perkins and Tony Rinaudo. Ruth was reaching out to villages, doing Bible teaching, and training volunteer village health workers. Tony was involved in many development projects, including Farmer Managed Natural Regeneration [Editor's note: This was featured in the chapter on the 1980s]. He also conducted research on edible seeded Australian acacias—testing different species for suitability and safety. Local women

were very innovative in creating new recipes incorporating the nutritious acacia seeds. MIDP agents, who were mostly Christians, worked closely with EERN evangelists in villages, and their influence and leadership led to the establishment of several small rural churches.

A Change in Government

On January 27, 1996, my wife, daughter, and I heard the rat-tat-tat sound of machine gun fire at the office in Niamey. The unfolding coup d'état ousted Niger's first democratically elected president, Mahamane Ousmane, after three years in power and installed General Ibrahim Baré Maïnassara as head of state. We stayed in close contact with the American embassy to create a contingency plan (thank you Jim Knowlton). There was fear that we would have to evacuate the country. This possibility created stressors that kept many of us awake at night. In the end, the coup was relatively peaceful, and no evacuation was necessary. One side note: Several weeks later we found a bullet which had come through a bedroom window and landed on top of one of our wardrobes. We still have the bullet!

Deaths

When we arrived in Niger in 1986, I had assumed that missionaries no longer died on the field. My assumption was proved wrong when a senior missionary and an MK went to be with Christ. Leonardo Navarra, a career missionary in Zinder, was called home in 1990. His Hausa name was Malam Murna (joy) since he was known for his joyful disposition. Leonardo had a youth ministry that was sanctioned by the local government, and which clearly had an impact in the lives of young Nigeriens. In 1991, one of our MKs went to be with her Good Shepherd. Little Emily Philpott, daughter of Pep (director at Galmi Hospital) and Dr. Jane Philpott, died from cerebral meningitis on her way from Maradi to Galmi Hospital. Her baby sister, Bethany, was very ill with the same disease so she and her parents were medically evacuated after a beautiful funeral service at Galmi. Thank God that Bethany had a full recovery!

A Vision for SIM-Niger

After an absence of 23 years from SIM, we went to Charlotte in January of 2022 for 10 weeks as volunteers. It was wonderful to spend time with four SIM-Niger couples that we had served with. We also saw Dr. Joshua Bogunjoko who remembered Carolyn and me, much to our surprise. While there, we learned that it is now difficult to find candidates who are willing to commit to long-term service. My vision and prayer for SIM-Niger is for the Lord of the harvest to call many young people who are compelled to stay the course that is needed for a significant impact among the various people groups in Niger.

My Reflections on SIM Niger's 100TH Anniversary Commemoration

Gordon Evans (1997-2007)

After a very productive and demanding term as Director of the new Niger Field, Nelson Frève and his family returned home. Graham Wiggett, Area Secretary, assumed the Field Director responsibilities for two years while Judy and I returned to Canada unexpectedly. We returned to Niger in December 1997 at which time I assumed the

Area Director role. I served one term as Deputy Director under Nelson Frève, and two terms as Area Director. It was a period of transition for the Field.

Under Nelson Frève's visionary leadership, SIM Niger's Field Administration reorganized into Ministry Focus Teams with the Team Leaders assuming much of the role formerly played by Station Managers. There were 12-13 specific teams working in administration, community development, health, education, gospel witness/discipleship, etc. This approach generated fresh vision, recruitment, and mobilization, particularly in the ethno-linguistic focus teams—Fulani, Manga, Songhai, and Tamajaq. Institutional teams also benefited, now enabled to recruit the appropriate personnel most needed.

Church relation responsibilities did not just multiply five-fold with four additional church partners, they exploded exponentially. Given the complications of balancing SIM Niger's new relationship and role with five church entities, the Niger Area Council meetings did not have church representation. This was a great loss for all parties. One of the first matters of business to tackle during my tenure was the Francophone Niamey Bible School's future, still jointly owned by the three SIM/Church entities of Benin, Burkina Faso, and Niger. Ownership matters were resolved after much discussion with all parties; however, for Niger, theological training at the Ecole Biblique in Niamey was lacking for the next several years. By God's grace, a new theological college, initially known as ESTEN and later to be called ESPriT, opened in September 2003.

During the 1990s, there was a profusion of new missions and denominations emerging in Niger. It became apparent that one clear voice was needed to represent the community of Evangelical Missions and Churches to the government and the public. In 1998 the Alliance des Missions et Églises Évangèlique au Niger (AMEEN) was established to do just that.

My first term recollections are mostly of attempting to adapt SIM Niger's Ministry Team approach to the vast and often remote placement of our missionaries. Member care and ministry coordination with other teams, as well as connecting and collaborating with local and national church representatives in that context were being stretched and needed attention. The lack of Area administrative presence in those areas, and the inadequacy to address those issues from afar necessitated adjustments. Unfortunately, the Field's new team structure worked so well that Field Administration needs were often left unmet because no one felt 'called' to those seemingly mundane roles in a time of exciting expansion everywhere. I was overwhelmed by too many responsibilities, many of which were far away, and there were not enough personnel to share the load. Judy and I went home in 2002 after my first term as Area Director totally spent, lacking emotional steam and energy, and devoid of vision.

My second term recollections are at the opposite end of the scale from the first. God gave us renewed strength, vision and courage. It was God, not us. God provided an Administrative Team with all the necessary experience, gifts and capacities to forge ahead effectively, truly thriving. Steve and Mikki Schmidt moved from Madaoua to Niamey to assume the Deputy Area Director position. Lucie Brown stepped into the role of administrative assistant. Other empty administrative positions were also filled. God's new plan for Judy and I was to take Wednesdays off from the office to fast and pray at home in the morning and meet one-on-one with pastor couples in the afternoon.

These meetings helped identify the priority strategic needs of our church partners:
- The need to strengthen Christian marriages and homes,
- Quality education for their children, and
- Revival in the Church.

[Editor's Note: You can read about what God did on the first two of these strategic needs in the chapters on the 2000s and 2010s.] Here is a little excerpt from the Evans' prayer letter of February 2004 on the third of these priorities:

> One of the key strategies that the Lord laid on our hearts was to make available to our churches the deeper life teaching of Canadian Revival Fellowship through Quebecois members Donald and Lorraine Gingras. We want to share with you that God answered [prayers] in wonderful and amazing ways in every one of the seminars and conferences across Niger. Their message of "Reconciliation with God and with One Another, the Path to Revival" has greatly impacted believers in every centre. The teaching on dealing with sin through confession, dealing with the self-life by bringing it to the cross and allowing the Spirit to reveal and deal with the specific roots of sin causing our recurring failures, then being filled to overflowing with the Holy Spirit, was a recall to some and a totally new concept to others.

Recollections of My Time as Country Director

Steve Schmidt (2007-2018)

Of all the experiences as director in Niger, the one thing that stands out from that time was the efforts made to rebuild trust with our church partners. The first meeting I had as director with the leaders of the five SIM-related church associations was concerning theological scholarships. It was clear from that meeting that we had work to do and there would be no quick fixes.

In June of 2009, a review team evaluated the ministries of SIM Niger. They wrote this in their final report:

> There is a widespread recognition of a poor relationship, distrust and suspicion between SIM and the churches. In addition, there is a perception that SIM and the church exist in separate spheres with little understanding across the barrier.

In 2011, there was an SIM leadership conference in Ghana. The church presidents along with the leadership of SIM Niger decided to charter a bus and travel together. It was one of the best decisions we ever made. With 30 hours going to Accra and 30 hours back, there was plenty of time to get to know each other in new ways. At the leadership conference, Dr. James Plueddemann taught on cultural differences. He told a story of a monkey and a fish who wanted to be friends but because their contexts were so different, they misunderstood what the other needed. Dr. Plueddemann's teaching sparked new understanding in our own situation. Dr. Joshua Bogunjoko shared a video entitled "The Problem of the One Story." We each tell a story about the other which isn't all false, but it isn't all true either. And these stories are passed from person to person and from generation to generation. In the bus on the way home, one of the church presidents said, 'I think a lot of our relational problems are explained in the teaching we received in Accra.' We decided we would be ambassadors of a new story. We would plan our own event that would allow more leaders to catch the new vision of unity.

We planned a weekend leadership conference at the Siloé Catholic retreat center outside of Niamey in January 2012. The theme of the conference was 'Rebuilding Trust.' We again invited Dr. Plueddemann. He again taught on cultural differences and told the story of the monkey and the fish. The teaching and the sharing together were excellent, but none of us expected what happened on Sunday morning—the last day of the conference. One of the church presidents stood up and said, 'We have some unfinished business. Over the years, I have been deeply wounded by SIM. But I have also wounded SIM. Today, I would like to ask for forgiveness.' He also apologized for his attitudes and actions toward the other church associations. When he finished, the other church presidents stood up one after the other and asked for forgiveness. I spoke last. I confessed that as director of SIM Niger, I was guilty of perpetuating the wrong story about my Nigerien brothers and sisters and I had influenced the attitudes of many of my fellow SIM workers. When I had finished speaking, the initial president approached me and gave me a huge embrace. We both had tears in our eyes. While we held this embrace, the group began to sing, *A Toi La Gloire* ('Thine be the glory').

Our next challenge was to share the message of rebuilding trust with the pastors of Niger. A pastor's conference was held March 2013 at Maza Tsaye Conference Center. Once again Dr. Plueddemann came. He again told the story of the monkey and the fish, and it was just as compelling as when he told it in Ghana. There were about 70 pastors in attendance. At the end of the conference, the church leaders, pastors, and SIM leaders made an agreement to walk in a spirit of reconciliation and mutual forgiveness. It was at this conference that the *Eglises en partenariat avec la SIM* (Churches in partnership with SIM or EPSIM) was born. EPSIM is a partnership of SIM-related churches that functions as a workgroup and forum for mission and church leaders to share ideas.

In December 2017, EPSIM organized a joint Christmas celebration. It would be the first time that all five SIM-related churches would celebrate Christmas together. The event was named Noël Ensemble (Christmas Together). During the service, the president of EPSIM retold the story of reconciliation and rebuilding trust going back to the beginning and the leadership conference in Ghana. In March 2018, the youth presented a concert at the *Centre d'Arts Martiaux*. Instead of having a choir from each church association, they formed one single choir. It was beautiful. Toward the end of the concert, one of the youth addressed the large crowd. He said, "We were not born when the main evangelical church in Niger divided, but as the Christian youth of Niger, we have never stopped dreaming of unity. The audience erupted in applause. One of the church leaders, leaned over to me and whispered, "This is the fruit of Siloé!"

To All Who Pray for Rain

Roger Stoll (2018-2022)

In less than a decade, we have seen huge changes in many West African countries. The dirty reality of terrorism has been rearing its ugly head, seemingly without restraint. Could it be possible that we have indirectly contributed to these changes? When we asked our Heavenly Father to act powerfully to redeem the lost in Niger, did we actually ask for trouble? Did our prayers for the coming of God's Kingdom stir up the spiritual climate in the nation? Did our intercession not only bring blessings but also incite opposition to the cause of Christ? I am convinced that our prayers for rain caused our feet to get muddy too.

These harsh new realities have forced SIM Niger to stop work in certain places, to rethink, and to adapt. But we have not abandoned our people, our ministries, or our churches. Despite the hardships, SIM has kept on working, looking for more ways to integrate missionaries from new sending countries, as well as national believers into our organization, to make Christ known in Niger.

To the new and seasoned missionaries and the EPSIM churches... what is to be done with the mud that comes with the rain? It is good to realize that mud is normal. In fact, it is to be expected when it rains. So, there is no need to get stuck in it, complain about it, or be afraid of it. Continue on, despite the obstacles. Move forward, by prayer, for the next hundred years in the knowledge that "The Son" burns bricks out of mud in the heat of affliction, to build His church in Africa.

Reflections on The Niger Centennial

Jonathan Moore (2022-Present)

Since I have been Director for less than two years, I wasn't sure what thoughts I had to offer. On further reflection, though, I realized that Bonnie and I served under every one of the four previous directors! Later this year, Bonnie and I will celebrate 30 years in Niger, which is almost one third of SIM Niger's history! I guess I might have some things to reflect on after all.

We arrived in Niger in October 1994 while Nelson and Carolyn Frève were on Home Assignment and Gordon Evans was Interim Director. The Frèves returned the following year, and we were here for the 1996 coup that Nelson refers to in his director's reflections. In fact, at the time of the coup, we were expecting our third child any day! I remember hearing Nelson's voice on the walkie-talkie immediately after the gunfire asking, "Where is Bonnie Moore?" Our son, Tim, was born a week later, while still under curfew restrictions.

Looking back over these 30 years, some things have changed tremendously in Niger, in the Church, and in SIM. We have seen enormous growth in technology in the world, including in Niger. This changes our communication and adds new methods of sharing the gospel. We've seen numerical growth in the church over these years which has also allowed SIM and the church to work closer in partnership and a shift towards more support and encouragement of the church in their ministry vision. At the SIM level, we've seen a shift in more short-term workers coming, offering both blessings and challenges.

However, in other ways, it seems like things have hardly changed at all. While the Church has grown numerically, there is still so much to be done, still so many people living and dying without having the opportunity to hear God's Good News. We need to harness the new realities we are living and continue to ask God's wisdom to know how we at this time and in this place can best continue to do His work.

When we first started talking about the centennial celebration, we had two scripture verses which we considered choosing for our theme. The first one was Hebrews 13:8, which became our theme. The other one was 1 Samuel 7:12 where Samuel sets up a stone that he calls "Ebenezer," meaning "Thus far the Lord has helped us." I pray that this centennial celebration year can be an "Ebenezer" stone for future generations, a testimony to God's goodness and faithfulness.

What a blessing to reflect on the last 100 years! Thus far the Lord has helped us! Let's not forget that there is still lots more to do and He who is the same yesterday, today and forever will continue to be our strength, our wisdom, and our salvation in what is to come.

A fitting conclusion and challenge as we end this book.

TIMELINE

Events Related to SIM Niger		World and Regional Events
	1920	
	1922	Transition of Niger from French territory to a French colony.
	1923	
Arrival of the first SIM missionary in Niger, Ed Rice.	End of 1923	
SIM buys property in Zinder, establishing the first mission base in French country.	1924	
	1926	The capital of Niger moves from Zinder to Niamey.
David & Drusille Osborne settle in Tibiri to begin ministry in this new location.	25 Dec 1927	
	29 Oct 1929	Beginning of the stock market crash in the United States, which leads to a decade-long, worldwide depression.
David Osborne, Ed Morrow, and Canadian businessman Henry Stock travel with Rowland Bingham across western Niger to Ouagadougou, Upper Volta, to survey Francophone Africa for ministry. This marks the beginning of SIM's work among the Gourmantché people.	Dec to Jan. 1930	
First baptisms in Tibiri.	1930	
Construction of the first church in Tibiri.	1931	
	1932	The colony of Upper Volta is dissolved, and the eastern half of the country is absorbed by Niger.
Start of the Touareg work under the Hodgsons in Zinder.	1934	
	7 Jul 1937	Japan invades China.
	1 Sept 1939	Germany and the USSR invade Poland.

Abba Moussa (Zinder) declares his faith in Christ.	1939	
Baptism of 14 people in Tibiri.	**1940**	
	10 May 1940	Germany invades the low countries and France. Capitulation of France on 22 June.
Start of SIM work in Maradi and Djirataoua.		
	July	French West Africa sides with Vichy France and Germany in World War Two.
Confinement of SIM missionaries to major centers.		
	1942	Death of Rowland Bingham, a founder and General Director of SIM from 1898.
		The Free French gain control of French-speaking West Africa.
	1944	Guy Playfair becomes General Director of SIM.
	8 May 1945	World War Two ends in Europe.
SIM begins work in Dogondoutchi. Construction of a dispensary in Tibiri.		Flooding in central Niger causes extensive damage and the relocation of Maradi and Tibiri towns to higher ground.
Opening of the Hausa Bible School in Tibiri.	1947	
Believers build a much larger church in Tibiri.		The colony of Upper Volta is revived, and the eastern part is split off from Niger.
SIM begins work in Madaoua.	1948	
Opening of Galmi Hospital.	**1950**	
SIM headquarters in Niger moves from Tibiri to Maradi.		
The French colonial government gives permission for SIMAIR to land in Niger, Dahomey, and Upper Volta.	1951	Libya gains independence from Italy.

SIM starts work at Soura and Tahoua.	1952	
Guéchémé Dispensary opens.	1953	
Dungas Dispensary opens.	1955	
Danja Leprosarium admits its first patients.	1956	Tunisia and Morocco gain independence from France.
The farm school starts at Maza Tsaye.	1957	Ghana becomes the first nation in West Africa to gain its independence.
		Albert D. Hesler becomes SIM General Director.
	1958	The French Community of Nations is formed, and Niger is granted autonomy from France.
EERN founded	1960 3 Aug 1960	Niger gains independence from France.
EERN recognized by the Niger government.	1961 31 Jan 1961	Assassination of Patrice Lumumba (Congo).
Beginning of SIM work in Maïné-Soroa	1962	Raymond Davis becomes General Director of SIM.
		Second Vatican Council.
Beginning of SIM work in Gouré.	1963 1964	Assassination of John F. Kennedy.
Opening of the Bible School in Aguié.		
	1965	End of the Second Vatican Council

	1966	Discovery of uranium in the Sahara.
Opening of the Tibiri Primary School.	1967	
	1968	Assassination of Martin Luther King, Jr.
	1969	First man on the moon.
	1970	
SIM Francophone office for Dahomey, Upper Volta, and Niger opens in Niamey, Niger.	1972	Abduction and killing of Israeli hostages at the Summer Olympics in Munich, Germany. Major drought in the Sahel.
SIMAIR sets up a base in Niamey.	1973	Arab oil embargo leads to inflation and an economic downturn around the world.
The Francophone Bible School moves from Mahadaga, Upper Volta to Niamey, Niger.	1974 15 Apr 1974	First coup d'état in Niger overthrows President Diori Hamani.
	1975	The Republic of Dahomey changes its name to the Republic of Benin Ian M. Hay become General Director of SIM.
SIM Niger welcomes its first missionaries from Asia, Dr. Andrew and Belinda Ng from Singapore.	1977	
	1979	Israel and Egypt sign the Camp David Accords. The Iranian Revolution results in the storming of the American Embassy and the taking of 52 hostages.
	1980 1981	Assassination of Anwar-al-Sadat in Egypt.

SIM Niger	Year	World
	1981 to 1985	Massive drought in Africa causes much suffering.
	1984	Assassination of Indira Gandhi in India.
Beginning of SIM work in Diffa.	1985	
SIM Niamey office moves from the Petit Marché to its current location near Tillabéri Road.		
Opening of Sahel Academy.	1986	
	1987	Death of Seyni Kountché, president of Niger.
	1989	Fall of the Berlin Wall, Germany.
	1990	Tiananmen Square massacre in China.
Division of the Niger church into three independent bodies: EERN, UEEPN, & UEES (Salama).	1991	
Government recognition of the EEI Church.		
Nelson Frève becomes director of SIM Niger.		
Beginning of SIM work in Téra.	1992	
Recognition of ACEN by the Niger government.	1993	James E. Plueddemann becomes SIM International Director.
		Signature of the Oslo Accords between Israel and the Palestinians.
	1994 Jan 1994	
Opening of SIM work in Nguigmi.		Devaluation of the West African cfa franc by 50%.
		Nelson Mandela elected president of South Africa.
		Genocide of Rwandan Tutsis.

SIM begins work in Dakoro.	17 Jan 1996	Overthrow of Mahamane Ousmane in the second coup d'état in Niger.
Gordon Evans becomes SIM Niger Director.	1997	
Formation of AMEEN.	1998	
Installation of SIM missionaries in Makalondi to start work among the Gourmantché.	19 Apr 1999	Assassination of President Ibrahim Baré Maïnassara of Niger.
	2000	Riots in Maradi bring destruction to churches and the SIM property.
Beginning of SIM work in Tchin-Tabaraden.	2001	
	11 Sept 2001	Terrorist attacks using planes kill almost 3000 people in New York, Washington, DC, and Pennsylvania.
	2002	
Opening of the Niamey Bible College (École Supérieure Évangélique de Niamey [ESTEN]), later to be called ESPriT.	2003	Malcolm McGregor becomes SIM International Director.
	2004	A devastating earthquake and tsunami in the Indian Ocean leaves over 225,000 dead.
Steve Schmidt becomes SIM Niger Director.	2007	
	2008	Financial crash in New York leads to "The Great Recession." Election of Barak Obama as the first black president of the United States.
Opening of the Fulfulde Ministry Training Centre. Accreditation granted to Sahel Academy.	2010	A coup d'état in Niger overthrows President Mamadou Tandja.

Opening of Danja Fistula Centre.	2011	
Meeting of church and SIM leaders at Siloé promotes reconciliation and forgiveness.	2012	
Niger River floods in Niamey.		
SIM begins work in Dioundiou.		
	2013	Joshua Bogunjoko becomes SIM International Director.
PAACS (Pan-African Academy of Surgeons) training begins in Galmi.		
	2014	Ebola epidemic starts in West Africa.
	2015	During riots across Niger, over 80 churches are burned and the SIM property in Gouré is destroyed.
Formation of EPSIM (Églises en Partenariat avec la SIM).	2017	
Roger Stoll becomes SIM Niger Director.	2018	
	2020	The COVID-19 Pandemic shuts down commerce and international travel around the world.
		Rounds of flooding in Niamey as the Niger River tops the dikes. Serious flooding in other part of the country.
		The murder of French tourists visiting the giraffes in Niger leads to restrictions on internal travel for foreigners in Niger.
Jonathan Moore becomes SIM Niger Director.	2022	
	2024	Phillip Bauman becomes SIM International Director.

ACKNOWLEDGEMENTS

As with any book of this kind, it would not have come to fruition without the input of a team of people contributing their gifts, their comments, and their ideas to improve the manuscript. Many thanks go to Beka Rideout and Nancy DeValve for their proofreading skills in checking the English manuscript and making suggestions for improvement. I also wish to thank Beka for her work on the SIM Niger timeline, a portion of which appears at the end of the book. Not only does the timeline help place the events of the book in order and in context, but it also serves as the inspiration for a few good stories.

As for the French version of the book, I used DeepL software to make an initial translation from English. While this helps with many aspects of translation, it is not sufficient or accurate enough to produce a correct, idiomatic translation in any language. To ensure accuracy and flow, Jocelyne Rowcroft served as translator of the text, taking the DeepL translation and comparing it to the original English text to craft a good rendition. Anna and Judicaël Marques then reread the translated French text, offering their suggestions and corrections. My deepest thanks go to all three for their careful and exceptional work.

Other people made important contributions to the development of the book. Four former directors wrote their observations and reflections on their time as SIM Niger Area Director, in the process relating engaging stories of their own. Jonathan Moore, the current director, added his thoughts. I also wish to thank Tounkara Maiyaldou, current director of the Theological College in Niamey, for his valuable reflections on SIM's work in Niger from the perspective of a leader in the Nigerien church. Thanks, too, to Joshua Bogunjoko, former director of SIM International, for contributing a foreword to the book.

A special note of thanks goes to Eric Wellborne, archivist at SIM International headquarters in Fort Mill, SC, USA. Eric helped facilitate two intensive weeks of research in the SIM Archives to find stories for this book, particularly from the early years. Eric guided me to important materials, pointed me in the right direction for others, and even uncovered a few hard-to-discover resources I had overlooked. Another SIM member who contributed to this book is Annabelle Lee. She developed the map at the beginning of the book so that readers would have a good idea where most of the places named in the book are located.

A big thank you goes to Amy Moore, who designed the cover of the book and assisted with layout and formatting of the text and pictures. Thanks, Amy, for volunteering your time and talent on this project to make it look sharp.

Of course, the book would not be complete without the contributions of many SIM Niger alumni, the children of former SIM missionaries, and some Nigerien colleagues. You contributed valuable and unheard stories about your lives in Niger. To all those who gave contributions, many thanks. There are many stories that did not get included, and I only wish I could have included every story and every word of what you wrote, but it would have made the book too long and too heavy.

Thanks again to all those who facilitated the research, writing, and publishing of this book.

John R. DeValve
john.devalve@sim.org
30 April 2024

BIBLIOGRAPHY

"A Short History of Tibiri Station," 1947. SIM Int'l.

Adolph, Harold Paul. *Surgeon On Call 24-7*. La Vergne: Christian Faith Publishing, Inc., 2018.

———. *Today's Decisions, Tomorrow's Destiny*. E. Spooner, WI: White Birch Printing, 1999.

———. *What If There Were Windows In Heaven*. Meadville, PA: Christian Faith Publishing, Inc., 2017.

Africa Now. "Cultivating New Ideas in Niger." June 1978.

Africa Now. "Farmer Evangelistis Graduate in Niger." 1968.

Asiwaju, Anthony. "Back Again at Draconian Border Closure Policy." *Punch*, August 29, 2019. https://punchng.com/back-again-at-draconic-border-closure-policy/.

"Autorisation d'atterir en AOF," juin 1951. SIM Int'l.

Beacham, George and Mae. "How God Answered Your Prayers: Niamey, Niger Republic." *Africa Now*, 1978.

Bingham, Rowland V. *Seven Sevens of Years and a Jubilee: The Story of the Sudan Interior Mission*. New York: Evangelical Publishers, 1943.

Bishop, Gordon, Gordon Beacham, and David Knowlton. "Pioneer Teams Survey Remote Tchad Basin." *Africa Now*, no. 5 (Apr-Jun) (1960): 6–8, 10–11.

Bishop, Lena. "Gordon Bishop's Death," November 2, 1984.

Bliss, Brian & Cathy. "News Updates." *SIMRoots*, 2010.

Bosch, Miriam Diez. "Niger: Their Enemies Burn Their Churches ... and They Forgive Them." *Aleteia*, April 11, 2015. https://aleteia.org/2015/04/11/niger-their-enemies-burn-their-churches-and-they-forgive-them/.

Botheras, Bev. Tell Everyone: A Story of One Man's Journey Faith, March 12, 2023.

Brant, Howard E. "Niger—Land of Standing Millet Stalks: A Report on SIM's Ministry in Niger, West Africa." Charlotte, NC: SIM International, June 13, 1988.

Burt, Jonathan. "SIM Literacy Work in Dosso Region." UK, 2023.

Casper, Jayson. "The Forest Underground: How An Australian Missionary Regrew the Sahel." *Christianity Today*, November 10, 2022. https://www.christianitytoday.com/news/2022/november/cop27-forest-underground-niger-trees-sim-creation-care-fmnr.html.

Chisolm, Elizabeth. "Lessons from Liz Chisolm." Charlotte, NC: SIM USA, 1988.

"Congo Nurse Now Serving in Niger." *Africa Now* (May-Jun) (1968).

Cooper, Barbara M. "Chapter 10: Maternal Health in Niger and the Evangelical Imperative: The Life of a Missionary Nurse in the Post-War Era." In *Transforming Africa's Religious Landscapes: The Sudan Interior Mission (SIM), Past and Present*, 287–312. Trenton, New Jersey: Africa World Press, 2018.

Cooper, Barbara M. *Evangelical Christians in the Muslim Sahel*. Bloomington, Ind: Indiana University Press, 2010.

Cowie, Chirs & Helen. "Education—Niger—Sahel Academy," September 8, 1986.

'Dan Nana. "A Letter from Dan Nana." Translated by Ray De la Haye. *Sudan Witness* XXIII, no. 3 (May) (1947): 15, 22.

DeValve, John R. "The Amazing Journey" Journal 11 (September 22, 1992).

———. "Trip to Galmi" Journal 7 (June 12, 1986).

Dipple, Bruce E C. "A Missiological Evaluation of the History of the Sudan Interior Mission in French West Africa 1924-1962." DMiss, Trinity Evangelical Divinity School, 1994.

Djibo, Moussa. "Moussa Djibo Testimony," March 3, 2023.

Dowdell, Howard. "Death of Roland Pickering." Letter, October 11, 1974. SIM Int'l.

"Drought Damage W. Africa Worsens." *Africa Now* Jul-Aug (1974): 10–11.

Eckert, Tim & Sue. Prayer Letter. "Eckert Extra." Prayer Letter, December 2000.

Edwards, Betsy. "Miracle at Mouzoumouzou." Niger, 1993. SIM Int'l.

Evans, Gordon. "AMEEN Signing," April 10, 1998. SIM Int'l.

Evans, Judy. "Académie Evangelique Cornerstone Maradi, the Crown Jewel of all the Maza Tsaye Ministries," August 9, 2023.

———. "Maza Tsaye Centre of Ministries—The Story of God's Amazing Goodness & Faithfulness," August 9, 2023.

"Famine." *Africa Now* Sept-Oct, no. 70 (1973): 8–9.

"Filmstrips Captivate Niger Muslims." *Africa Now*, no. 46 (Sep-Oct) (1969): 14.

"French West Africa." *Sudan Witness* XVI, no. 5 (Sep-Oct) (1940): 24.

"From Tsibiri," September 1945. SIM Int'l.

Fuller, Harold. "Hospital on the Edge of Nowhere." *Africa Now*, no. 33 (Apr-Jun) (1967): 6–7.

———. *Run While the Sun Is Hot*. New York: Sudan Interior Mission, 1967.

Haaga, Bert. "Operation Outcry." SIM Niger, September 1994.

———. "Prayer Letter," November 1999.

Hall, John F. "Farthest West." *Sudan Witness* V, no. 3 (Nov-Dec) (1932): 11–12.

Heikkila, Josh. "Muslims Stand with Christians against Attacks on Churches in Niger." *Presbyterian Church (USA) News*, February 25, 2015. https://www.pcusa.org/news/2015/2/25/muslims-stand-christians-against-attacks-churches-/.

"History of Tibiri Station," 1933. SIM Int'l.

Hodgson, Kenneth O. "Men of the Veil." *Sudan Witness (British Edition)* VII, no. 3 (Nov-Dec) (1960).

———. "Visit to a Touareg Camp." *Sudan Witness* IX, no. 3 (Nov-Dec) (1935): 19–20.

Hooker, Dave. "The Aussie Forest Maker Helping to Heal the Planet." *Eternity*, November 5, 2021. https://www.eternitynews.com.au/world/the-aussie-forest-maker-helping-to-heal-the-planet/?fbclid=IwAR013490joI8NNVSH5KCohgybZIaEejuY76oFKX4_WtUbiFHzow97t61GfE.

I, T. "Recollections of a Fulani," July 23, 2023.

Interview with Ed Morrow, July 1985. SIM Int'l.

Janssen, Sarah, ed. *The World Almanac and Book of Facts, 2022*. New York, NY: World Almanac Books, 2022.

Johnsen, Pete and Jackie. "Newsletter," October 1992. SIM Int'l.

Kapp, Newton. "Survey in French West Africa." *Sudan Witness* XXIX, no. 1 (Jan) (1953): 19–20.

Kephart, Thelma. "Ray and Sophie de la Haye: 41 Faithful Years." *Intercom*, October 2009, 165 edition. SIM Int'l.

Kirk, H A. "Obituary for Marguerite Morrow." *Sudan Witness* XXIV, no. 1 (Jan) (1948): 12–13.

Kopp, John. Recollections of George and Mae Beacham, February 12, 1988.

Larson, Immie. "A Discussion of Church Growth Among the Hausa People of Niger," December 31, 1995.

Long, Ruth. *A Family Living under the Sahara Sun*. Bloomington, IN: Xlibris Corp., 2011.

Lovering, Kerry. "Deep Roots." *Africa Now*, no. 18 (Jul-Sep) (1963): 8–9.

———. "Lena, It's About Gordon." *SIM NOW* Mar-Apr, no. 20 (1985): 5.

———. "Man with the Big Back Yard." *Sudan Witness* XLII, no. 3 (Jul-Sep) (1966): 2–4.

———, ed. "Missionary Dies in Crash." *Africa Now*, no. Nov-Dec (1974): 11.

———. "Niger President Decorates Mission Leader." *Africa Now*, December 1969. SIM Int'l.

———, ed. "People of the Wilderness." *Africa Now*, no. Jan-Feb (1975): 4–5.

———. "Rugged Life Among the Tuareg." *Africa Now*, no. 59 (Jul-Aug) (1970): 3.

———. "The Nomad Tuaregs, Islam's Lords of the Desert." *Africa Now*, 1978. SIM Int'l.

———. "You Bought It, You Wear It." *SIM NOW*, 1986.

Lyons, Bill. "Can You Trust a Smuggler?" *SIMRoots* 36, no. 2 (Fall 2019): 13.

Mahamane, Addo. "Chapter 8: History and Challenges of the Evangelical Church in Niger, 1923–2013: The Case of the Evangelical Church of the Republic of Niger (EERN)." In *Transforming Africa's Religious Landscapes: The Sudan Interior Mission (SIM), Past and Present*, 225–58. Trenton, NJ: Africa World Press, 2018.

Morrow, Edward. "Beginnings of SIM Work at Zinder, Niger," January 31, 1987.

Morrow, Edward M. "Abba Musa of Zinder." *Sudan Witness* XXII, no. 4 (Oct) (1946): 19–22, 24.

———. "Recollections of Mr. Edward Morrow, Sudan Interior Mission, Missionary to Niger 1930-1945," 1980.

Ng, Belinda. "An Integrated Model of Member Care—Niger," July 11, 2023.

"Niamey Bible School," 1980. SIM Int'l.

"Niger Church Statistics." AMEEN, February 2017.

"Niger: SIM OK after Coup." *Africa Now* Jul-Aug, no. 75 (1974): 11.

Nomaou, Ibrahim, and John R DeValve. Tsibiri dans les années 1930-1970. Face-to-face, February 3, 2024.

"Obituary for Charles Zabriskie," December 10, 2001.

"Obituary for John Ockers," January 5, 2017.

"Obituary for Mr. E. F. Rice." *Sudan Witness* XVI, no. 1 (Jan-Feb) (1940): 15.

"Obituary for Ralph Kenneth Ganoe." *Sudan Witness* XXIV, no. 6 (Nov) (1948): 7–8.

Ockers, John. "History of SIM Work in Niger—1923-2000," 2005.

Osborne, David and Marie. "Prayer Letter," August 1949. SIM Int'l.

Osborne, David M. "Outline of Mission Work in Niger Colony." *Sudan Witness* XXII, no. 4 (Oct) (1946): 7–10.

———. "Travelling in French Sudan." *Sudan Witness* V, no. 1 (Jul-Aug) (1932): 8–11.

———. "Tsibiri Flood Report," August 11, 1945. SIM Int'l.

Osborne, Drusille. "Letter from Drusille Osborne to Mr. and Mrs. Trout," February 11, 1929. SIM Int'l.

———. "The Growth of the Sunday School at Tibiri." *Sudan Witness* VI, no. 5 (Mar-Apr) (1934): 12–14.

Paternoster, Dan. "Report of October 1993 Mission," February 20, 1994.

Paterson, Barbie. "Stories from the Patersons," July 6, 2023.

Pieké, Michelle. "Moving Toward Hope: Physiotherapy at CSL+DFC Danja," July 26, 2023.

Playfair, Guy W. "Demande d'autorisation de résider dans le Cercle de Maradi," May 18, 1927. SIM Int'l.

———. "Obituary for Drusille Osborne." *Sudan Witness* XVII, no. 1 (Jan) (1941): 3–4.

———. "Retrospect and Prospect." *Sudan Witness*, 1936.

Potratz, Randy. "Jim Rendel and the Very Hot Day," July 31, 2023.

———. "Lizard for Lunch," July 31, 2023.

———. "Speech, Speech, Speech at the FEU," July 31, 2023.

Rice, Edward F. "A Trip in the French Sudan." *Sudan Witness* IV, no. 6 (Jul-Sep) (1925): 22–23.

———. "Zinder." *Sudan Witness* V, no. 3 (Nov-Dec) (1932): 11–12.

Rideout, Ian. "Report on Air Rescue," May 2023.

Rinaudo, Tony. "The Development of Farmer Managed Natural Regeneration." *Leisa Magazine* 23, no. 2 (June 2007): 32–34.

———. "The Discovery of FMNR," April 3, 2023.

Schaffer, Rich. *Just One SIMAir Story*. Bloomington, IN: iUniverse, 2012.

Schmidt, Mikki. "Accreditation of Sahel Academy," October 30, 2023.

Schmidt, Steve. "Reflections on the History of SIM in Niger." Powerpoint presented at Orientation, Niamey, NIGER, October 2015.

"SIM Helps Famine Victims in East and West Africa." *Africa Now* Nov-Dec (1973): 9–10.

SIM NOW. "Danja, An Eternal Healing Touch." Winter 1994. SIM Int'l.

SIM NOW. "Sai Galmi." 1993.

Simms, Alberta. "SIM Niger in the 1940s," December 4, 1992. SIM Int'l.

Sivakumar, M V K. *Le Climat de Niamey*. Niamey, NIGER: Centre Shélien de l'ICRISAT, 1986.

St Germaine, Eugenie. "Inusa—Man of God." *Sudan Witness*, 1955.

Starke, Joe. "The Beginnings of PAACS," March 8, 2024.

Strong, Susan. "Building Walls." June 2, 2023.

Swanson, Alan. "Death of Gordon Bishop," October 25, 1984.

Tashibka. "An African Letter." Translated by Ray De la Haye. *Sudan Witness Supplement II* 3 (May) (1949): 3.

Truxton, Charles. *The Quiet Passion Behind the Stones.* Jos, Plateau State, Nigeria: Geovany Digital Creative Prints, 2023.

"Uranium Find in Niger Republic." *Africa Now,* no. 35 (Oct-Dec) (1967): 13.

Van Lierop, Gwen. "Cut and Polished." *Africa Now,* December 1964. SIM Int'l.

VerLee, Jim. "VerLee Letters," n.d.

Wall, Martha. "Help Those Women." *Sudan Witness* XXIX, no. 2 (Mar) (1953): 7–9.

———. "Prayer Letter," 1946. SIM Int'l.

———. *Splinters from an African Log.* Chicago: Moody Press, 1960.

Watt, Milton. "Ministry of Milton and Linda Watt in Niger," July 31, 2023. Email.

World Health Organization. "Leprosy (Hansen's Disease)," 2023. https://www.who.int/data/gho/data/themes/topics/leprosy-hansens-disease.

World Watch Monitor. "70+ Churches Destroyed as 'Anti-Charlie' Protests Spread in Niger." January 20, 2015. https://www.worldwatchmonitor.org/2015/01/70-churches-destroyed-as-anti-charlie-protests-spread-in-niger/.

Younge, Nigel. "SIM in Niger: the origins and development of an Evangelical Protestant church in Muslim West Africa." University of Chester, 2015.

Youssoufou, Oumarou. "Come ... But Live Among My People." *Africa Now,* no. 60 (February 1972): 6.

Zabriskie, Marcia. *A Challenge from the Sahara.* Niger, 1984.

Made in the USA
Columbia, SC
25 October 2024